THE SIMPLE ART OF
LETTING GO

THE SIMPLE ART OF
LETTING GO

Daily Mindful Practices to Move Beyond the Past, Claim Inner Peace, and Find Your Path to Emotional Freedom

LILA HART

Copyright © 2024 Lila Hart - All rights reserved.

The content contained within this book may not be reproduced, duplicated or transmitted without direct written permission from the author or the publisher.

Under no circumstances will any blame or legal responsibility be held against the publisher, or author, for any damages, reparation, or monetary loss due to the information contained within this book, either directly or indirectly.

Legal Notice:

This book is copyright-protected. It is only for personal use. You cannot amend, distribute, sell, use, quote, or paraphrase any part, or the content within this book, without the consent of the author or publisher.

Disclaimer Notice:

Please note the information contained within this document is for educational and entertainment purposes only. All effort has been executed to present accurate, up-to-date, reliable, complete information. No warranties of any kind are declared or implied. Readers acknowledge that the author is not engaged in the rendering of legal, financial, medical or professional advice. The content within this book has been derived from various sources. Please consult a licensed professional before attempting any techniques outlined in this book.

By reading this document, the reader agrees that under no circumstances is the author responsible for any losses, direct or indirect, that are incurred as a result of the use of the information contained within this document, including, but not limited to, errors, omissions, or inaccuracies

Table of Contents

Introduction 1
Free Bonus: Bridging the Gap 4

Part 1: Letting Go of the Past — 6

Chapter 1
Understanding Trauma 7

Chapter 2
Cultivating Forgiveness 23

Chapter 3
Embracing Impermanence 31

Part 2: Romantic and Platonic Relationships — 38

Chapter 4
Recognizing Signs of Toxicity 39

Chapter 5
Honoring Your Boundaries 51

Chapter 6
Embracing Grief and Loss and Moving On 57

Part 3: Your Inner Critic — 68

Chapter 7
Understanding the Inner Critic 69

Chapter 8
Cultivating Self-Compassion 77

Chapter 9
Challenging Negative Self-Talk............................. 85

Part 4: Your Identity — 94

Chapter 10
Exploring Self-Identity...................................... 95

Chapter 11
Embracing Authenticity 103

Chapter 12
Letting Go of Labels....................................... 109

Part 5: Beyond Control — 118

Chapter 13
Surrendering to Uncertainty 119

Chapter 14
Trusting the Process....................................... 127

Chapter 15
Embracing Surrender 133

Part 6: Untangling Your Emotions — 142

Chapter 16
Recognizing the Complexity of Emotions 143

Chapter 17
Embracing Vulnerability and Authenticity................. 155

Chapter 18
Finding Meaning and Growth in Emotional Challenges..... 163

Conclusion 171

What if the task is simply to unfold, to become who you already are in your essential nature—gentle, compassionate, and capable of living fully and passionately present? How would this affect how you feel when you wake up in the morning?

–Oriah Mountain Dreamer

Introduction

"Just let it go!"

Four powerful words indicating something is over, no more, in the past, and yet, the pain and agony attached to "It" is still very much a present matter to you.

They're often said before someone storms off after a heated argument, perhaps even slamming a door or rushing off with screeching tires.

Perhaps these four words are what everyone tells you when you struggle to overcome some kind of tragedy. Maybe the voice uttering them is only in your mind; as you know, letting go is the best thing, the *only* thing you can do, if only you knew how.

Letting go is only hard when you have to let go of something that means a great deal to you. If it doesn't mean anything to you or impact your life to a great extent, letting go is as easy as pie, and you don't even think twice about it. But when it isn't easy, and it does mean a great deal to you, letting go can leave you in a pickle, and you'll remain stuck in one place until you're able to *let it go*.

Sadly, for some, this may never happen. But it doesn't have to be the case for you. If you're keen on transitioning your life to enjoy the freedom letting go brings to you and are willing to do what it takes, then you're standing on the precipice of a breakthrough. You're about to turn the page on whatever is keeping you stuck in life. It equates to taking the first step toward realizing your full potential in life.

The Art of Letting Go covers the process of letting go of six notoriously hard things to let go of.

- ✧ The past and the trauma it inflicted on your life
- ✧ Toxic romantic or platonic bonds
- ✧ Your inner critic persistently whispering nasties into your ear
- ✧ Your idea of yourself, your identity, and being unable to embrace who you are
- ✧ The loss of control and not being able to impact matters beyond your reach
- ✧ Toxic emotions poisoning you from the inside

While every part offers helpful guidance and advice, the layout of the book enables you to jump to the parts applicable to your life story and the challenges you're facing.

Be prepared to find that once you let go of one particularly pressing matter, another area demanding your attention will reveal itself. This is because the process of letting go is sometimes structured in layers, and as you peel away the most pressing matter, the next falls in line to be addressed. It is only complete once you reach the core of your existence, from which healing and growth will sprout. Then, you enjoy ultimate freedom of mind, body, and soul, enabling you to achieve your full potential.

My hope is that every part of this book encourages you to dig deeper into the reality of your state, enabling you to take a step back to change your perspective so you can ultimately see that it isn't as much about letting go as it is about realizing what is already gone. Every word captured is done with the intent of inspiring you to take the very first step of holistic healing and to continue making persistent progress until you arrive at your destination.

May this be a happy and enlightening journey!

Free Bonus
Bridging the Gap

Before we get into the main body of the book, I have some gifts for you. One of the main concerns with self-help books like this is that it is so easy to read the book, but it is much harder to take the knowledge you've gained and apply it to your life. Change is only possible when knowledge is put into practice.

Let's be real with each other for one last time: How many self-help books have you read and while the content amazed you and revealed new opportunities to live your best life, you never thought about what you'd learned once you put the book down?

I can say that this has happened more than once to me, and I truly think we're all guilty of it.

Don't worry, it's not your fault. It can be hard to take the lessons of others and apply them to your unique circumstances. It is why I included this bonus session, a **5-day challenge**, to get you going and give you some momentum, making it much easier for you to keep doing what is right for you.

Inside this challenge, you'll discover:

- **The area(s) of your life you need to let go of.**
  You may already have an answer in your mind when you purchased this book, but I promise you the exercise we are about to work on might reveal something else that surprises you.
- **One simple mental shift you can do to turn your mood around.**
- **The fundamental principle of letting go** – discover this, and you will set yourself free from the mental jail that you put yourself in.

Simply go to: https://empowermindpublishing.com/Free-Gift-Letting-Go or scan the QR code

Part 1

Letting Go of the Past

We're starting our quest to *let go* with retrospection and by addressing the pain of past experiences to enable you to embrace the present. This chapter explores how holding onto past hurts and regrets can hinder personal growth and inner peace.

Chapter 1

Understanding Trauma

People find it difficult to let go of their pain. They prefer familiar suffering because they fear the unknown.

—Thich Nhat Hanh

It's hot and humid. Lubang's climate can be daunting, draining every drop of emotional, mental, and physical energy from locals and visitors alike. Yet the harshness of the jungle and the climate of the island are the last things on the minds of the group of soldiers under the guidance of Second Lieutenant Hiroo Ononda of the Japanese Imperial Army. They've been stationed on the small island in the Philippines since December 26, 1944, almost two months ago now.

The trauma they've witnessed is too hard for the minds of those accustomed to the comforts and luxuries of modern Western life to fathom. We'll never truly understand what the young intelligence officer, soon to turn 23, had witnessed. World War II was in its final stages, and calling the situation grim for the Japanese would be a vast understatement, especially since the American soldiers had stepped onto the island with absolute force.

Many of Ononda's fellow soldiers have been killed. Others surrendered. Only Ononda and three of his men managed to escape into the jungle. From here, they'd positioned themselves to continue the fight with guerilla warfare. It was an atrocity to humanity, and the young Ononda wasn't merely witnessing the onslaught of his people but was fighting at the core of the action.

Ononda was a trauma victim, but even when the war was over, the pain and agony of warfare didn't end for him. The pain and suffering caused by war —the discomfort, displacement, and persistent pursuit of the enemy he chose to hang on to— became a familiar agony, a suffering he couldn't let go of.

Hiroo Ononda became a soldier who didn't stop fighting. The group of four continued to attack supply lines, shoot soldiers, and fight the local population. Hiding in the jungle, he didn't know about the atomic bombs on Hiroshima and Nagasaki. He didn't know the war was over. His commitment was to fight the war that had displaced him in the first place. He chose to ignore any and all attempts to bring him back from his place of agony. Every attempt to lure him out of the jungle and into the light failed. The U.S. Army flew planes over the jungle, dropping leaflets and asking soldiers in hiding to come out as the war was over. Ononda didn't budge.

'It's a trap,' he thought.

The Philippine government tried to extract these soldiers from the jungle but failed. In 1952, the Japanese government made another attempt to remove Ononda and more soldiers like him from the Pacific but failed.

Years went by. There were no more shootings, no more trauma, no more leaflets, and still, Ononda stayed tucked away in the jungle, persistently fighting and clinging to his pain. For him, it wasn't over by choice. There were no enemy forces left on the island, and now his onslaught was against innocent people. Locals were murdered, livestock stolen, and farms burned down.

In October 1972, private 1st Class Kinshichi Kozuka, Ononda's last comrade in the battle, died. Ononda was left alone with his misery and pain. A new world existed that he knew nothing of. His endurance in holding on to the trauma imposed on him is astounding.

Only in 1974, the year he turned 53, did he step out of hiding and surrender. Nothing could bring him peace. Ononda refused for too long to let go and set himself free from the pain of past trauma.

Are you still holding on to a war that no longer exists? Do you find comfort in the familiarity of the pain trauma brings? Are you hurting those around you and ignoring outside attempts to relieve your pain? Can you see yourself, your life, and your story reflected in the lost life of Hiroo Ononda?

The Burden of Past Trauma

The first question essential to address in our search for freedom from the impact of past traumatic experiences is: What is trauma? The simplest definition of the term would be to call it exposure to an event or a series of events, either as a victim or witness, that was deeply emotionally disturbing. However, when digging deeper, we have to recognize a few important characteristics of trauma relevant to the quest to let go and unburden ourselves.

The first is that trauma occurs in a *state of disempowerment*. Dr. Peter Levine, the founder of the Somatic Experience, describes trauma as the experience of fear in the face of helplessness.[1] Being disempowered in the moment of fear multiplies the powerful impact of the event, turning it into a phenomenon devastating for the human psyche.

It is a unique experience. There are different types of traumatic experiences, like exposure to abuse, neglect, rejection, and poverty. Yet, we need to recognize

---

1   Poole Heller, D. (2020, July 29). *Types of trauma and identifying the signs.* Trauma Solutions. https://dianepooleheller.com/touching-on-trauma/#:~:text=According%20to%20Peter%20Levine%2C%20the

early on that the type of traumatic experience doesn't carry as much weight in understanding the impact of trauma as the individual perception of the event does. Dr. Nicole LePera, founder of The Holistic Psychologist, explains that the impact of trauma is nestled in our unique experience of trauma rather than in the nature of the event itself. It is why the same traumatic experience can have an entirely different impact on all who have witnessed it. She also expands by saying that because trauma is such an individual experience, it isn't always an obvious event.

The final point I want to highlight about trauma is that it is often linked to the *betrayal of the self in order to gain love and acceptance* while being treated as unworthy or unacceptable. Dr. LePera expands on this attribute of trauma by explaining that this notion establishes a mindset supporting the need to betray yourself in order to gain love and acceptance. This betrayal turns into a means to survive.[2]

The Impact of Trauma

Psychological analysis over many decades leads us to conclude that exposure to trauma results in an array of impacts on our holistic wellness. I am specifically referring to matters like sleep disorders, increased anxiety levels often serving as the onset of depression and other mental health concerns. Trauma victims are more likely to suppress their emotions and avoid feelings, locations, and activities that could serve as triggers to relive the trauma they have experienced. They are tired from having frequent nightmares even as trauma flashbacks taunt them while awake.

Yet, for me, the true tragedy centers around losing your life. Not through death, though all of the above contributes to a much higher risk for suicide, but by never truly living. By the time Ononda stepped out of the jungle, his

---

2   *Top 30 Nicole LePera quotes (2024 Update)* . (n.d.). Quote Fancy. https://quotefancy.com/nicole-lepera-quotes

prime years had passed. His dreams were never realized, and his relationships with his loved ones were forgotten. What was he suffering for? Clinging on to past trauma equates to hurting loved ones, hurting ourselves, and missing out on life as the years pass by in vain.

Trauma can take on many forms and can occur at any stage of life, though it occurs most commonly during the childhood years. Statistics reveal that as many as 60% of the adult American population has had at least one adverse childhood experience (ACE), while about 15% have had four or more ACEs in their lifetime.[3]

An even more alarming concern is intergenerational trauma, when the impact of past experiences extends beyond one lifetime and becomes the heritage passed on to the next generation. Being a victim of such trauma leaves you in a different kind of pickle for distinguishing yourself, as the pain conveyed to you is often disguised as normal, making it harder for you to interact with the world. It is the kind of trauma that Dr. Mariel Buqué describes in her book *Break the Cycle: A Guide to Healing Intergenerational Trauma* as follows:

> "Intergenerational trauma is a wounding of the soul. It's a multilevel emotional injury that impacts a person's mind (their thoughts and emotions), body (the way they carry suffering physically), and spirit (a disruption in their inner knowing and connection with others)."[4]

---

3   *Unwrapping the Link Between Childhood Trauma and Health.* (2021, January 20). EndCAN. https://endcan.org/2021/01/20/unwrapping-the-link-between-childhood-trauma-and-health/#:~:text=Approximately%2060%20percent%20of%20Americans

4   *Buqué, M. (2024). Break the Cycle. Penguin.*

While Dr. Buqué's description is specifically aimed at explaining intergenerational trauma, her words capture the essence of past trauma and the impact it has on every part of your being. Refraining from letting go of past pain impacts every aspect of your existence, now and in the future, shaping your identity accordingly.

Exploring Coping Mechanisms

In Dr. Bessel van der Kolk's bestseller, *The Body Keeps the Score: Brain, Mind, and Body in the Healing of Trauma*, he explores how traumatic experiences impact the brain. These experiences are at the root of several chemical and functional changes in the brain structure, specifically in the emotional centers of the brain, which is the brain stem and limbic region. These changes demand the need for coping mechanisms to overcome the challenges that past trauma presents in order to let go of the impact of these experiences so that you can enjoy life. While we'll be exploring several healthy coping mechanisms, it is important to note that there are also many unhealthy coping mechanisms that can have an even more detrimental impact on your life. I am specifically referring to matters like substance abuse, alcoholism, abusive behavior, isolation, overworking, and even denial.

Before we explore some of the most effective coping strategies to process unresolved trauma, it should be mentioned that the success of any of these mechanisms depends on understanding why you're stuck in this state. This will become easier once you realize that the trauma occurred during a state when you felt helpless and that you're *no longer* disempowered and can break free from the grip of unresolved trauma. Then you can make choices about the approach you want to take and gradually start to let go of the pain. Reclaiming your power will also help you to let go of any unhealthy coping mechanisms your mental stability may be leaning on and replace them with healthy strategies.

Consider that coping strategies need to address both the triggers activating your trauma response as well as the traumatic event itself to help you let go of past traumatic experiences.

Steve Havertz, the clinical director at Highlands Springs, offers some inspiration for expanding your toolbox and developing effective strategies for overcoming unresolved trauma in your life. The following are all helpful techniques from his collection of aids to add to your life survival toolkit

Breathing Techniques

Taking deep, deliberate breaths is one of the simplest and most effective ways to immediately bring about a state of deeper calm and relaxation. Why is that?

Let's have a quick look at the vagus nerve's function to understand why breathing exercises are so effective. It is part of the body's parasympathetic nervous system and is responsible for controlling several life-sustaining actions like heart rate, breathing, and immune response. These are all functions impacted during high-stress periods and are functions you have no control over. That is, except for breathing. You can make a conscious decision to slow down your breathing, which will instruct your vagus nerve to slow down your heart rate, resulting in lower blood pressure and bringing about a greater sense of overall calm. So, effectively, by changing your breathing, you can claim control over various bodily responses toward stress to induce a state of calm and take your body out of high stress. Hence, breathing techniques have been a helpful aid dating back centuries and have been used to bring about deep relaxation and improve stress management. A 2019 study determined that breathing exercises, specifically yogic breathing, improve anxiety, depression, and sleep problems while also addressing a range of other serious health concerns.[5]

---

5 Hoshaw, C. (2022, January 31). *How conscious breathing can help relieve anxiety and stress.* Healthline. https://www.healthline.com/health/mind-body/conscious-breathing#benefits

Entering such a trancelike state of calmness can also help to release traumatic memories and the emotional responses accompanying these moments. It provides a medium to clear yourself from toxic emotions impacting every aspect of your life.

There are numerous breathing exercises like box breathing, 4-7-8 breathing, and belly breathing, to name only a few. Each of these offers various benefits, and I encourage you to research and practice several methods until you've found the breathing technique that best addresses your needs.

One breathing technique I would like to expand more on, as it delivers many exciting results and is one of my preferred options, is biodynamic breathing.

Biodynamic Breathwork

Biodynamic breathwork eases emotional pain, supports spiritual connections, and helps to heal trauma and depression. This breathing exercise takes place in a standing position, so find a comfortable stance with your feet hip-width apart. But if you're not comfortable standing for some time, you can sit or lie down. Just ensure you're in a comfortable position, allowing for freedom of movement.

1. Play some background music or use headphones. Relaxing music, like natural sounds used for meditation, works best.
2. Close your eyes and shift your attention to your body.
3. Slowly inhale and exhale through your mouth. Try to keep the same rhythm without pausing.
4. Once you're comfortable, start moving your head, jaw, and face in ways with which you feel comfortable in the moment. Opt for free movement without the need for pattern or repetition.
5. Maintain this position for a few breaths, and then begin to rotate your shoulders and arms.

6. Gradually, add movement to more body parts, working your way down through your hips into your legs and feet.
7. Keep the movements simple, unorganized, and free.
8. Notice how your body lights up, feeling alive. If you experience any discomfort, like trembling or tingling, move through them slowly until they dissipate.
9. Continue moving and breathing for as long as you like and enjoy the moment of deep calm.

Are you ready to immerse yourself in a state of calm?

Other highly recommended breathing techniques serving as aids to deal with past trauma are holotropic breathwork and the Wim Hof method.

Holotropic Breathwork

In the 1970s, Dr. Stanislav Grof and Christina Grof developed holotropic breathwork, a technique consisting of fast breathing and evocative music to induce a state of consciousness and calm in which healing can take place. It is known for initiating higher levels of consciousness, improving post-traumatic stress, and reducing depression, and is often used in treating drug addiction.

It is best practiced with the guidance of a facilitator or with online support. Evocative music is an essential element of this type of breathing and should be played in the background.

1. Find a comfortable position to lie down in, closing your eyes.
2. Breathe deeply through your mouth without pausing between breaths.
3. Continue this rather rapid breathing pace while shifting your focus to the music.

4. Become aware of any feelings that may surface and express them through either sound or movement of your body while remaining lying down.

5. Once you reach a state where these emotions and movements are freely connected, you've entered a state of connection with your inner intelligence.

6. Remain in this state until your facilitator gently guides you back to a state of relaxed consciousness.

The Wim Hof Method

In recent years, Wim Hof's popularity has been on the rise as 'The Iceman'. This extreme sportsman pushes the barriers of endurance through his specialized breathing techniques, enabling him to achieve the seemingly impossible. The specific breathing technique helps to keep you within the window of tolerance. Dr. Dan Siegel identified a zone within which you can function optimally and named it the window of tolerance.

The specific breathing technique relies on oxygen-rich breathing to oxygenate the body. The entire process has many physical benefits, but what makes it particularly interesting and helpful in dealing with trauma is that it increases stress tolerance while making it easier to accept the present. It induces a higher state of safety and calm.

1. Lay down or sit in a comfortable position with closed eyes.
2. Inhale through your nose and exhale through your mouth, ensuring every breath is a large gulp of oxygen rich air pulled into your belly.
3. Repeat these short but powerful breaths between 30-40 times.
4. Exhale on your last breath, then inhale deeply, holding your breath for as long as possible.
5. Exhale and inhale, holding your breath for only 15 seconds.

6. Go straight into the next cycle, repeating the entire process three or four times.

7. Be aware that the rapid increase in oxygen in your blood can leave you feeling light-headed, and it is best to remain in a seated or lying position.

While breathing exercises bring many benefits, it is essential to remember that your body isn't used to this high level of oxygen. Therefore, it is better to refrain from practicing these powerful breathing techniques if you're facing health challenges like high blood pressure, epilepsy, cardiovascular disease, have a history of panic attacks, or are pregnant.

Mindfulness Exercises

We have discovered that traumatic experiences become trapped in the body as a result of research by Bessel van der Kolk and other specialists in the field exploring the body's reaction to trauma. The mind doesn't know how to process these experiences and stores them away. It follows a kind of out-of-sight, out-of-mind regime. However, as these feelings or responses to events are both foreign and toxic, the body rejects them. Lately, research exploring the connection between these stored negative experiences and disease is on the rise, leading us to realize that putting up with these emotions can be detrimental in the long run. If this is a topic you would like to explore, I encourage you to follow the work of Dr. Henry W. Wright. His book, *Exposing the Spiritual Roots of Disease,* forms part of an entire collection exploring this link from a religious perspective. Similarly, Dr. Caroline Leaf's books are also hugely insightful, as she expands in great depth on how feelings, past experiences, and negative thinking can not only keep you trapped but also induce various severe health concerns.

However, there is also a secondary concern I want to address: how these feelings cause a sense of disconnection with the body, called dissociation.

Dissociation serves as a defense mechanism to protect the mind from these entrapped feelings. Mindfulness exercises enable you to overcome this gap and reconnect your mind, body, and spirit so that you can be whole as a person. Mindfulness exercises have been proven to be effective in reducing stress and increasing resilience. The best part is that while you can work with a therapist to release these emotions, you can also practice them at home.

Essentially, anything you fill your days with can turn into a mindfulness exercise, and the more you focus on being mindful, the longer you'll remain in a mindful state. The longer you're in this state, the more you'll feel connected with your body, reduce the sense of dissociation, and reduce stress and anxiety.

Let's be mindful right now.

1. Grab an apple or any other fruit of your choice.
2. Look at it. Can you distinguish different color tones on its skin? What does the surface of the fruit look like? What texture does the peel have? Now, sniff it. How would you describe its aroma?
3. If you have to peel the fruit first, do so now. Explore the inside texture and color while doing so. Notice the juice of the fruit running over your fingers. Or, just bite into the fruit. Is it crunchy, juicy, or soft? What words would you use to describe its texture?
4. What does it taste like? Do you like the feeling of its texture on your tongue? Is it sweet? Think about the fruit in as much detail as possible.
5. Consider where it was grown, how it was harvested, and the journey it had to take to get to you. Give thanks to all who were involved in the chain, from the farmer who nurtured the plant to the person who sold it to you.

6. In this moment of awareness of the present moment, you're mindful of not only the fruit but also your body and the effect eating it has on you. You are connected, focused, and, may I say, more relaxed?

You can repeat this exercise as many times as you like during the day. When showering, notice the sensations of the process. When on the subway, notice the people around you, what they wear, what you see, and how it all makes you feel.

Alternatively, you can also practice mindfulness as a form of meditation by finding a comfortable spot where you can be undisturbed. Take slow, deep, and deliberate breaths, and focus on your breathing and how the air passing in and out of your body makes you feel. Or you can listen to music, shifting your focus to what you hear, the lyrics and melody, and how hearing the song makes you feel.

Including Fun in Your Life

As kids, our minds were persistently seeking ways to have fun. Growing older, having fun becomes a mere memory, as society seems to frown on adults having such experiences. Just think about how long it's been since you last had fun. Can you even remember what you did? Did you play? Most likely not. Play is no longer part of your life experience, is it?

Yet, experts in trauma recovery are highlighting a growing awareness of the importance of play and fun as mediums to deal with unresolved trauma. Even when it doesn't feel normal any longer to seek out moments filled with fun and play as an adult, these moments encourage a sense of vitality. They make you feel alive, like your days have meaning and your life has a purpose.

Engaging in fun and play increases serotonin levels, improving your mood. Fun and play can boost your energy, improve your sleep quality, and lower stress levels. These are all factors that strengthen your ability to cope with trauma and the stress associated with unresolved traumatic experiences.

Mark Twain referred to laughter as *the only weapon the human race has*, while others call it the *best medicine*. Weapon or medicine, we know having fun makes us feel better. Studies also reveal that scientific evidence supports this statement and that it is far more than a mere hunch.

There are three prominent psychological theories surrounding the use of humor as an aid to relieve emotional distress.

- The *relief theory* sees humor, laughter, and fun as a form of tension relief. When internal negative energy, like what you experience from unresolved trauma, builds up, it does the same to your mental state as what a build-up of steam would do to a pipe. Pressure mounts until the weakest part of the pipe gives way, causing a burst; internal pressure is relieved, but damage is created and, in some cases, casualties. Fun offers relief as it lowers the pressure and prevents a devastating mental explosion.

- The *superiority theory* offers another perspective on the role of fun as an aid to improving self-esteem. Think back to the last time you laughed at someone else's mishaps. Perhaps it was something they said or did that was silly. How much better than them did you feel when you burst out laughing? The humor we see in other's mistakes makes us feel better about ourselves.

- The *incongruity theory* looks at how the human mind expects things to happen in a certain order, so when the unexpected breaks this order, it's funny, breaking the tension and causing a disruption in negative thought patterns. An example of such an unexpected twist is the joke punchline.

All of these theories deliver valid arguments to consider fun and play as possible coping mechanisms to deal with unresolved trauma.

But what is fun?

Since fun is an individual experience, instead of offering a definition, I want you to explore what fun means to you.

While the idea of what is fun should've evolved over time, the reality is that for many adults, especially if you're dealing with unresolved trauma, fun didn't evolve: it went extinct. Below are some questions to bring your fun experiences to the surface. Allow these questions to entice your mind to think about fun once again.

- ✧ What events or activities make you smile, laugh, feel joy, contentment, or excitement?
- ✧ Do any of these events or activities lean toward being a source of play, meaning they're no longer moments of accidental fortune, but can be deliberately engaged in?
- ✧ If you still struggle to fathom what fun would look like in your adult life, ask around what others do to have fun or recall the things you considered to be fun during your childhood years.
- ✧ How can you incorporate such activities into your daily routine, enabling you to engage in fun as an aid to deal with your unresolved trauma?

Include these activities and see how you can change them around to bring laughter, fun, and play back into your life.

Other effective coping mechanisms include expanding your support network, researching success stories, and allowing others' experiences to inspire you.

Practicing these techniques will help you progress to the next stage of letting go, a level called forgiveness.

It is where complete freedom from negative emotions and their grip on your life becomes a reality—a level possible only through sincere forgiveness of others and yourself.

Chapter 2
Cultivating Forgiveness

When we are no longer able to change a situation, we are challenged to change ourselves.

—Victor E. Frankl

7 April to 19 July 1994 was a bloody time in African history. This period was tragic and gruesome. The Rwandan genocide claimed between 500,000 and 800,000 lives, leaving many more injured, traumatized, and in despair.

Left to Tell by Immaculee Ilibagiza offers a small window for understanding the conditions survivors endured.

"I heard the killers call my name.

"They were on the other side of the wall, and less than an inch of plaster and wood separated us. Their voices were cold, hard, and determined.

"'She is here... we know she's here somewhere... Find her— find Immaculee.'

"There were many voices, many killers. I could see them in my mind: former friends and neighbors who had always greeted me with love and kindness, moving through the house carrying spears and machetes and calling my name" (Immaculée Ilibagiza & Erwin, 2014).

The book is her recollection of the attack on her country by its own people, but it is far more than that. She chose to move beyond the grip of trauma and share her story of forgiveness and hope. *Left to Tell* is a story touching on the complex nature of forgiveness and why it is so essential to pursue.

Forgiveness is a concept that is difficult to understand and even harder to practice. It is an entirely voluntary process that can't be forced, and yet, at times, there may be no other way to escape to freedom without forgiveness. Forgiveness may be the only way to free yourself from the grip of trauma. It may be the only way to escape its hold and regain your life. That is how it was for Immaculee Ilibagiza; she had to forgive and move beyond; otherwise, she was no better off than the thousands who died during this dreadful genocide.

The Healing Power of Forgiveness

The *presence of trauma always results in the need for forgiveness*. This is comprehensive forgiveness directed toward the party causing the trauma in your life, yourself for allowing it, or, in most cases, both directions. Forgiveness is the key to breaking free from the control your negative emotions, caused by exposure to trauma, have on you. It is the only way to let go of the pain, anger, and mounting hostility caused by these events, which prevent you from living fully while simultaneously causing your relationships to break down.

The process of forgiveness is far more comprehensive than merely forgetting about what has happened or quitting your anger. It is a process demanding and inspiring complete transformation. It can't be forced, but once you take the next step in this voluntary process, you'll gradually notice a change in your feelings, behavior, thinking, and approach toward life. As compassion for yourself and others and generosity become more prevalent in your life, resentment and bitterness will no longer dominate your life, choices, and thoughts.

Forgiveness occurs in stages.

- **First stage:** During this stage, *anger is still on the surface.* While this is highly disruptive to your life and relationships, it becomes even more toxic if you suppress the emotion. Hence, the best way to address this stage and progress to the next is to acknowledge what you're feeling and be transparent about your emotions.
- **Second stage:** Now, you've progressed from merely *acknowledging your feelings* to identifying the parts of your life and identity that you've lost through the traumatic experience.
- **Third stage:** This stage is all about *accepting the losses*. It is about awareness and acknowledging that certain parts of your being are no longer there without judging yourself or others for what has happened to your identity.
- **Fourth stage:** Finally, you'll be *ready to forgive* those who inflicted the trauma and be able to move forward, relying on your inner strength, skills, and resources to do so.

It is a process consisting of making progress and stepping back again. You may go forward and backward several times, but as long as you persevere, the freedom that complete unconditional forgiveness brings will be yours.

The Distinct Difference Between Forgiveness and Condonation

The term 'condonation' indicates that wrongdoing is no longer considered, and a blind eye is turned toward the action. It implies that a wrongdoer is pardoned through the act of condoning, that their bad or harmful actions are either not challenged or no longer seen as bad.

This is not the same as forgiveness. Forgiveness is very clear about the fact that what happened was wrong and is still recognized in that light, but a conscious decision was made to let go of the hurt and anger it brought into your life. It implies a willingness to treat the offender as if they're no longer guilty of what has caused emotional wounds, with the primary purpose of moving forward either in your relationship with the person who had to be forgiven or with your life.

Condoning often results in making excuses for a wrong. Forgiveness continues to acknowledge the wrong for what it is but lets go of the emotions it caused.

For instance, if your partner is cheating on you, and you're aware of this but not saying anything about it, you're condoning their behavior. While you may be condoning the wrong and refraining from taking any counteraction, like breaking up or getting a divorce, you haven't forgiven the person for their betrayal and the emotions it caused you to feel.

Let's say you find out your partner is cheating, confront them, and either decide to stay together with the help of a relationship counselor or get a divorce. You may choose to forgive your partner or ex-partner, allowing you to restore your inner peace and be able to have a civil conversation with the other person, as you may share kids. You also choose not to refer to the past and what they've done, but that never means you approve or allow such behavior.

Cultivating Forgiveness

You can't control who will come knocking on your door, but you can decide who you will let in and who you will welcome to sit down at your table.

Life is often unpredictable. There are lots of things we simply can't control, but there are also many things we have control over, and trauma can stem from either. However, how you manage the impact of trauma and how long you want to hold onto the emotional burden it caused, which can only be shed through forgiveness, is completely within your control. But as forgiveness directed toward oneself or others remains a challenging quest, it is a task much easier said than done.

Harnessing Sympathy Toward the Other

Let's start by exploring probably one of the most challenging exercises for forgiveness: sympathy. While it may be hard to fathom how you would ever be able to feel even a grain of sympathy toward the person who has hurt or angered you, it remains the most effective strategy to enjoy the freedom forgiveness brings.

Empathy is what you feel towards someone whose suffering you understand, sparking you to feel compassion toward that person. Sympathy is different Unlike empathy, it doesn't entail placing yourself in that person's situation, as you remain focused on how you perceive what they must be feeling. Sympathy is what you feel when you look at suffering from the outside, and is more like pity or compassion.

For instance, an emotionally neglected child may find forgiveness toward a parent who has rejected them once they understand that their parent was facing various emotional challenges themselves. The rejection and emotional neglect aren't dismissed through forgiveness. But the emotional burden that the neglected child, perhaps now an adult, carries is shed as it is possible to pity or sympathize with the transgressor. This makes it easier to understand that their behavior, words, or actions were rooted in poorly managed emotional burdens they were suffering.

Once you seek to understand what caused the behavior that invoked trauma in you, it becomes easier to sympathize, and through this sympathy, you can set yourself free through forgiveness.

Diluting Injustice

Greater injustice demands greater forgiveness. As a victim of injustice, your perspective on the severity of what you've gone through depends on where you stand in relation to what happened. According to Beata Souders, a positive psychology practitioner, changing this perspective can dilute the injustice and make it easier to practice forgiveness. Explore the injustice you need to forgive to determine whether there are any other ways you can perceive the matter, leading to a dilution of the injustice and making it easier for you to find forgiveness within.

Alternatively, she also suggests that it helps to lower expectations of what is believed to be the ideal outcome. Let's say your forgiveness is based on the expectation of an apology, but that apology never comes. How will you ever be freed through forgiveness if this expectation you have is too high, perhaps not feasible at all? Her suggestion is to expect less of those guilty of injustice to help yourself experience the freedom forgiveness brings.[1]

Disrupting the Neo-Associationistic Response

Rumination, a term used to refer to pondering past trauma, sets off a negative mental chain reaction. Have you had an experience where you thought about an unpleasant event, and the anger inside of you just started

---

1   Souders, B. (2019, August 29). *24 Forgiveness Activities, Exercises, Tips and Worksheets*. Positive Psychology. https://positivepsychology.com/forgiveness-exercises-tips-activities-worksheets/#how-to-be-forgiven n-7-actions-we-can-take

to brew like a volcano ready to erupt, locking you into a pattern of obsessive thinking? While it is frustrating when it happens, I want you to know you're not alone and that this phenomenon is common enough that it inspires deeper psychological exploration.

Dr. Leonard Berkowitz developed his Cognitive-Neoassciationistic Model (CNA) model back in 1989. Since then, the model inspired much additional research exploring the connection between frustration and aggression.[2]

The CNA model is based on the understanding that exposure to more unpleasant experiences leads to a greater response when anger is triggered. But when the same anger trigger is present, coupled with more positive experiences, the anger response is less severe.

Beata Souders refers to a similar chain reaction of emotions and the severity at which it occurs when she explains that rumination stimulates the rise of negative emotions linked to the memory of the specific transgression you need to forgive. To encourage and support the process of forgiveness, you have to short-circuit these negative thoughts. The moment you become aware you're in a state of rumination (which becomes easier to detect through mindfulness, sparking greater awareness), you need to break the chain. Shift your awareness back to the present to avoid increasing the negativity associated with a past transgression. Maintaining a positive outlook is much easier when you're in a state of greater awareness of the present moment. Revert to the mindfulness techniques shared in the previous chapter to help you move your mind from past to present.

Adopting these three strategies can form the backbone of your forgiveness, as they offer the necessary structure to support success in this regard. But I

---

2   Yarwood, M. (n.d.). Cognitive-Neoassociationistic (CNA) Model. *Psu.pb.unizin.org*. https://psu.pb.unizin.org/psych425/chapter/cognitive-neoassociationistic-cna-model/

am not ignorant of the fact that each of these strategies can be demanding in their own right. So, I encourage you to also explore self-care strategies, find a support network, and use journaling as a tool to shed your emotions and keep track of your progress.

Chapter 3
Embracing Impermanence

It is not impermanence that makes us suffer. What makes us suffer is wanting things to be permanent when they're not.

—Tich Nhat Hanh

Julia Samuel, author of *This Too Shall Pass: Stories of Change, Crisis and Hopeful Beginnings*, set the stage for her profound text with the following:

"An early English citation of 'this too shall pass' appears in 1848: When an English sage was desired by his sultan to inscribe on a ring the sentiment which, amidst the perpetual change of human affairs, was most descriptive of their real tendency, he engraved on it the words: 'And this, too, shall pass away.'"[1]

Today, the well-known phrase is commonly used to provide instant comfort during times of hardship, yet the true value it holds remains hugely

---

1   Samuel, J. (2020). *This Too Shall Pass*. Penguin UK.

underestimated. Change is an inevitable aspect of life. Knowing that bad things or situations will come to an end offers hope. Similarly, knowing that good things will also end at some point may serve as an encouragement to remain more present and appreciate things more for as long as they're part of our reality.

Samuel continues to explore the idea that, while change is an undeniable trait of life, it is still often perceived as dramatic, impacting our lives so negatively. I certainly find that change is perceived much more as something negative than something that can bring about a positive outcome.

Coupled with no self and nirvana, impermanence is one of the three Dharma Seals, the foundation of Buddhist teachings. Exploring impermanence from this perspective reveals that it is about far more than the understanding that all things will come to an end. Impermanence also means that nothing remains the same. Similar to a river where the same water will never flow past twice, the impermanent state of life assures that nothing can have a fixed identity because all things are constantly changing. This truth is also the reality of past trauma. As time goes by, nothing will change about the event or events that occurred. Yet, as you yourself are of a changing nature, your perspective on what happened will change. This is a natural process—a truth about nature's character. But you have the power to either resist the change or speed it up to step into your freedom sooner.

Impermanence is often met with sadness and is a cause of distress for many, but we should never forget that there is much more to it. "Thanks to impermanence, everything is possible. Life itself is possible. If a grain of corn is not impermanent, it can never be transformed into a stalk of corn."[2]

---

2   Nhất Hạnh, Thích. (2003). *No death, no fear : comforting wisdom for life.* Riverhead Books.

Impermanence Sets the Stage for Positive Transformation

Resistance to change is an exhausting and futile waste of time. You can't fight nature, regardless of how hard you try. But, once you peek beyond the conventional understanding and see past the perceived threat nestled in impermanence, it becomes evident that this ever-changing state forms the foundation of positive transformation.

Look around you. Every second, things are changing. The pace at which the earth is turning may be so slow that you don't always notice how the sun's position is changing, but after a while, it shifts from early morning to noon to sunset. You may not notice the color of the leaves changing until the early autumn breeze blows a blanket of orange, gold, and brown down the street. You may not notice the seconds passing until several minutes have gone by. And you may not notice how your body ages until one morning, you look in the mirror and spot gray hairs or wrinkles.

Change is always happening, both outside and within. As with external changes, you may not notice the transformations, maturity, personal development, or deeper compassion forming over time until you realize one day that you're no longer the same person you used to be.

It is a topic Eckhart Tolle expands on in his book *A New Earth: Awakening to Your Life's Purpose* when he says that once we acknowledge that everything in life is unstable and always changing, there comes a deep peace inside. Then, you realize you are fluid by nature and can develop beyond previously presumed boundaries and capabilities. In this moment of change, letting go of the past becomes an achievable quest, a medium to achieve ultimate freedom.[3]

---

3   Tolle, E. (2006). *A New Earth*. Penguin.

Mindfulness Practices to Embrace Impermanence

Designing your life to embrace and utilize a state of impermanence to your benefit and to enable you to let go of past emotional burdens demands a deep state of mindfulness. This is a state of existence encouraged through regular mindfulness practices.

Mindfulness forces a deeper awareness of the present moment and what is happening in your mind and surroundings. It keeps you fixated on the present and prevents past regrets or future worries from getting you off track.

It is in this state of mindfulness and being awakened to experience the present moment that you'll be able to lay down your emotional burden by letting go of past trauma to set yourself free. In this section, we'll go over a few mindfulness practices to help you get started.

The Observer Meditation

This specific meditation technique will help you disengage from your thoughts and feelings. It effectively creates the necessary distance to view past trauma from a different perspective. You can also use observer meditation to create a division between your challenges and your identity, as our challenges are so easily confused with being a part of who we are.

1. Find a comfortable position in a spot where you can sit without distraction or disturbance.
2. Breathe deeply as you settle into your mind and body.
3. Acknowledge the present thoughts and then clear them from your mind.
4. Shift your focus to your immediate environment. Visualize yourself sitting in this position but see yourself from a distance as an outsider.
5. Then, shift your focus to the inside. You're inside your skin. Aim to feel your skin not by touching it with your fingertips but by increasing awareness of its existence.

6. Imagine that the chair you are sitting in is supporting your structure while your skin gives shape to your being.
7. Notice the physical sensations and what they make you aware of at this very moment.
8. As soon as you become aware of a specific sensation, acknowledge it and gradually move on to the next.

Thoughts and feelings may surface during your meditation. Don't deny their existence, as that will only make them more persistent. Rather, acknowledge them, realizing you are an entity separate from your thoughts. The meditation technique helps you become comfortable with observing only you and who you are without any feelings or thoughts taking you off course.

Three Steps to Mindfulness When Time Is Limited

Mindfulness and all its benefits as an aid to letting go of the past are absent as long as you linger in autopilot mode. This mindfulness technique brings you out of autopilot and into awareness of the present.

Stop what you're so busy with and step into a dignified posture. While holding this pose, notice your thoughts and feelings before letting them flow through you. Then, move back into the moment and accept your current state of existence.

Hone your focus on one area of existence: breathing. Breathe in deeply, taking six breaths per minute. Notice the air entering and leaving your body, how it changes your muscles and shape, and how it feels to inhale and exhale. Use this heightened awareness of your breath as an anchor to remain mentally present in your physical state.

In the third step, you're expanding your awareness as you become increasingly aware of your body. Notice any stiffness, discomfort, aches, or pains you may feel. Considering your body as the vessel taking you through life and enabling you to live fully, determining the state of your vessel. Once you've acknowledged every bodily sensation, you can expand your focus even further onto your environment and notice shapes, patterns, sounds, scents, and textures in your immediate surroundings before gradually returning to your normal state of being.

The mindfulness exercises shared are best practiced daily at a set time and place. However, becoming more mindful, staying in the present, and letting go of your attachment to the past can be practiced during almost any daily routine activity. Revert to chapter one to refresh yourself on how to incorporate mindfulness into your daily routine tasks, and once you do, list ways you would like to turn ordinary tasks into mindfulness activities.

A Final Thought on Part One

Trauma has an overwhelming effect that can have a lasting impact on your life. But you don't have to remain in a state of disempowerment.

- Allow a deeper understanding of how trauma burdens you to encourage you to take the necessary action toward the freedom you want and deserve.

- There are many healthy coping mechanisms to deal with past trauma, and I encourage you to research these techniques to an even greater extent than what I explained. But remember that a small act in the right direction is far more powerful than a thousand good intentions, so try at least three different healthy coping mechanisms to determine what works best for you.

- Forgiveness brings freedom. Acknowledge who you need to forgive for what, and let forgiveness start to set in.

- Life is always changing. That is one certainty you can hold onto. While you can't keep things the way they are, you can determine in which direction you want to change. Visualize the destination you want the impermanent state of life to take you to.

Toxic relationships are one of the most prominent causes of traumatic experiences. The next chapter sheds light on toxic relationships, how such relationships poison your entire identity, and, of course, how you can let go to enjoy freedom!

Part 2
Romantic and Platonic Relationships

I dedicate the second part of the book to those who are navigating the challenging process of letting go of relationships that no longer serve their well-being. Whether you're at a breaking point and looking to end a relationship or are experiencing the pain of one being ended, this chapter will offer valuable insights and strategies for finding closure and healing.

Chapter 4

Recognizing Signs of Toxicity

You make me feel like a firefly. Trapped in a bell jar; starved for love.

—Ayushee Ghoshal

In 2011, Gotye released their album, Making Mirrors. It was almost an instant success. The song *Somebody That I Used to Know* was blasting across all radio stations. Its global popularity turned it into a hit, making the album a well-deserving winner of the Grammy Award for Record of the Year.

Lines like, "You can get addicted to a certain kind of sadness," or, "Told myself that you were right for me, but felt so lonely in your company," got stuck in our minds.[1] Perhaps songwriters Luiz Bonfà and Wouter De Backer (Gotye) were merely creative masterminds, or perhaps they knew the words captured the essence of toxic relationships, a phenomenon Forbes magazine

---

1 *Somebody That I Used to Know.* (2011, July 5). Genius. https://genius.com/Gotye-somebody-that-i-used-to-know-lyrics

informs us is present in the lives of at least 80% of all Americans.[2] Whether it is in friendship, familial bonds, or romantic relationships, our generation seems to be no stranger to toxic bonds.

The song could also easily be the soundtrack to the very infamous love affair between Lord Byron, a well-known poet and lady's man, and Lady Caroline Lamb, an accomplished novelist.[3] Their illicit relationship was characterized by immense highs and lows. The couple was notorious for bringing out the absolute worst in each other, to the extent that after Lord Byron insulted her in the middle of a public argument, Lady Lamb smashed a wine glass and slashed her own wrists with the shards. Later, she re-directed this destructive energy at Lord Byron directly by burning an effigy of him in front of an audience of local villagers, turning her feelings toward her ex-romantic partner into a public display. As shocking as it might have been, this was not where the toxicity ended. History books describe her feelings toward Lord Byron as an obsession that drove her to more bizarre actions, like spreading rumors about him and his half-sister, trying clumsily to blackmail him, and even writing her first book, *Glenarvon*, as a scathing critique of Byron's character. All the while, she was still writing him passionate love letters and desperately trying to see him. While she wrote that he was "mad, bad, and dangerous to know," Byron was telling his friends that he felt as though he were being haunted by a vengeful specter. Lady Caroline Lamb died as a result of her obsession, drinking and drugging herself into oblivion and physical illness.

---

2   Beheshti, N. (2020, May 15). *Toxic influence: An average of 80% of Americans have experienced emotional abuse*. Forbes. https://www.forbes.com/sites/nazbeheshti/2020/05/15/an-average-of-80-of-americans-have-experienced-emotional-abuse/?sh=6a7fda2f7b49

3   Sgnt, J. (2021). *6 Toxic couples from history*. Humans. https://vocal.media/humans/6-toxic-couples-from-history

Sometimes, more often than we would like to admit, crappy relationships fester, causing infatuation to turn into venom, killing your soul from the inside unless you let go.

Acknowledging the Red Flags

My grandma used to say, "Honey, nobody is as blind as the person who doesn't want to see." There are many instances in life where this saying rings true. Sadly, it is often the case that one of these instances is when you're trapped in a toxic relationship. While it is a terrible situation, many find acknowledging their situation to be a far greater threat than staying stuck in misery. Often, this may be because they see no other option than to remain put, or even more often, it is the case that the unknowns associated with freedom are far more daunting than the familiar pain they're so used to. While staying may seem to be the easier choice, you're only causing yourself far greater mental and emotional agony and harm, which eventually spills over to impact your physical well-being, too.

Perhaps a reminder of how harmful being in a toxic relationship, specifically a romantic relationship, is what you need to hear today, and we'll cover that in far greater depth in the next section. For now, let's first explore the many red flags indicating a state of toxicity, as that will assist in removing any doubt from your mind about the nature of your romantic bond.

It Goes Deeper Than the Obvious

Manipulation, the absence of trust, and emotional abuse are some of the most common perceived red flags associated with relationship toxicity. However, there is so much more to explore, and the first thing to know is that there are *different types of toxic relationships.*

- ⬥ *Over-dependency.* Initially, it may be endearing when your partner turns to you to make a final call on every decision to be made. However, while you make all the decisions, you're also solely responsible for the outcome when your choices don't go as planned. All the while, your partner is not taking any accountability. Soon, you'll realize that it is not a sustainable state for any bond, but once this dependency has turned into the norm for your bond, it can be very hard and even impossible to change the situation.

- *A poor-tempered partner.* Being in a relationship with someone struggling to manage their temper is immensely harmful to your emotional and mental well-being. It is the kind of relationship that can easily spin out of control, putting your physical well-being and safety at risk.
- *Users.* This toxic partner will see how much they can drain from you. While they don't make any deposits to support the emotional, physical, or financial state of your relationship, they'll make as many withdrawals as possible until you're completely drained.
- *A possessive partner.* Again, initially, your partner's jealousy might have made you feel loved and cherished, but jealousy, more often than not, has an ugly side that becomes unbearable to live with. When jealousy turns into possessiveness, you may find yourself being interrogated about your every move. Eventually, you become distant from friends and loved ones and may end up in a very isolated place. Often, it is this isolation and the lack of access to a support system that contributes to staying in this toxic state.

Can you see that it may be much harder than you thought to positively identify the toxic behavior you may be exposed to in your relationship? Even if your partner doesn't physically abuse you, living in an unstable and emotionally unhealthy environment can be just as bad.

10 Easily Missed Red Flags

According to Maggie Martinez, a licensed clinical social worker based in Arizona, there are as many as 45 red flags indicating a toxic relationship.[4] Some of these may be less obvious than others, but they're all detrimental to any relationship. She compiled an extensive list, but I want us to pause at the following 10 red flags. I find these 10 red flags easy to miss, making it so much harder to identify and acknowledge the toxicity in your relationship. Since it is only through awareness and acknowledgment that you'll be able to make progress to improve your life, it is essential that we explore these 10 signs in greater depth.

1. *You're just not happy in your relationship anymore.* I am a strong advocate of the statement that you have to be happy within yourself and not look to your partner to make you happy. However, being in a relationship should expand your happiness, as you should be getting support, encouragement, and acceptance from your partner. Your relationship should form a safe space where you're allowed to let your hair down and where you can make memories that expand your happiness.

2. *Every misunderstanding has to turn into a drama*, and arguments become explosions of hot words that hurt each other or get back at them. Eventually, there is nothing good left to hold onto as you destroy your relationship bit by bit. Dr. Scott Haltzman, author of the book *The Secrets of Surviving Infidelity*, states that toxic couples often thrive on moments of high theatrics.[5] These are moments of screaming, excessive hand gestures, wild accusations, and emotionally

---

4   Pace, R. (2024, March 28). *45 Warning signs of a toxic relationship*. Marriage . https://www.marriage.com/advice/relationship/warning-signs-of-a-toxic-relationship/

5   Haltzman, S. (2013). *The secrets of surviving infidelity*. The Johns Hopkins University Press.

charged words flying. Let's just be clear about one thing: such behavior isn't indicative of immense passion; it is pure poison. You are finding yourself in a toxic relationship.

3. *Your relationship lacks the backbone of reliability.* Can you rely on your partner to be there for you, no matter what? The reliability I am referring to goes beyond knowing they'll be there to assist when you need them; it also refers to knowing how they'll respond when having a difficult conversation is necessary. Can you trust your partner to talk to you, even when it is hard? Can you count on them to work with you through challenging feelings and situations in your bond without being left with feelings of abandonment or judgement?

4. *Feeling inferior in your relationship* isn't only a red flag that you may be in a toxic bond but also that you're highly likely trapped in this state with a narcissist. A narcissist typically presents with a sense of superiority, and they derive pleasure and satisfaction from leaving others feeling inferior to them. While they only do this to mask their own insecurities, it can be detrimental to the mental and emotional well-being of anyone sharing a life with them. Can you trust your partner to give you honest but uplifting feedback, regardless of the situation you present them with? Or, do you shy away from getting any feedback, as you're too familiar with the oncoming wave of confidence-destroying criticism?

5. "Every time I think about going home to him, I get the same sense of claustrophobic anxiety as when an elevator door closes behind me." I ran into my friend while waiting at the bar for my table to be cleared. She was sitting and having a drink all by herself, working up the courage to go home and face her life partner of three years. We've had many social events together and I knew them both quite well. While I never thought they would grow old together, I didn't

know what a bad state their relationship was in. What I learned that night from my quick chat with her is that *a toxic relationship leaves you feeling trapped and that often nobody else understands the severity of your situation,* as it is so easy to hide your hurt from others, even those close to you.

6. My aunt was a lovingly sweet old lady with whom I could have the most pleasing conversations about almost any topic I could think of. She was graceful and elegant, and I thought she was very wise. Her husband was a real gentleman. He loved being outdoors and spent many hours in the garden. He always said that he found peace with his fingers in the soil. Two lovely people, as long as they weren't in the same room. The moment you had them together at a family gathering, they turned into a toxic bomb ready to explode without considering who would witness the devastation they left or how ugly they became when they were going at each other all the time. *Toxic partners form a bad combination.* Individually, they can be the nicest people, but when together, they bring out the worst in each other.

7. Can you hear the eggshells crack underneath your partner's feet? Irritating right? Well, if that is the case, then it is time to ask yourself why it is that your partner feels the *need to be walking on eggshells.* Why is it that they have to adjust their behavior or words not to offend you? Why are you so easy to offend, and what makes it such a bad thing if you're offended? They're humans too and deserve the respect and acceptance to be their authentic selves, at least when around the person they're in a relationship with. Or, are you perhaps the one treading lightly, desperately trying not to crack any shells? Either way, see the red flag, as only once you acknowledge the state of your relationship can you start to let go or actively work towards a healthier and happier situation.

8. *Excessive focus on your shortcomings.* Is your partner painfully aware of all your weaknesses and always ensures you never forget about your shortcomings while they're evidently unaware of your strengths? Failing to see, acknowledge, admit, and appreciate your strengths is surely a red flag you need to be aware of.

9. Keeping you from spending alone time with your friends or family is another sneaky indicator of relationship toxicity. In every healthy relationship, there are times you spend together as a couple and times you need to do your own thing. However, if you find that your partner is often off doing their own thing while you're never spending time without them when hanging out with your friends or family, there should be a question mark in your mind. Determine whether it is a sign of commitment or if you have been robbed of your privacy. By all means, it may be that you just like to do things together all the time, that is, if it works both ways. But if you're noticing more red flags or feel a deep sense of discomfort in your bond, then it is far more likely that *your partner is invading your privacy* and robbing you of independent access to a support network.

10. Are you still taking care of yourself? Do you invest time into making sure you look good? When relationship toxicity levels rise, *self-care often takes a back seat.* Partners don't feel like they want to look good for each other anymore, and hence, they don't invest time in self-care habits and routines anymore.

These red flags make up only a small percentage of all the warning signs indicating a toxic state. Mostly, these aren't signs typically associated with toxic relationships, and that is exactly why I chose these 10 red flags to share. I want to demonstrate the complex nature toxic relationships can have and that it may be much harder to accurately determine the state of your relationship without mindful awareness of how you're feeling as a partner in this bond. Nevertheless, even if you're in denial or simply unaware of the severity of your relationship, this toxicity can have a far-reaching impact on your overall well-being.

Exploring the Deep Impact on Your Mental and Emotional State

Nobody is exempt from being entrapped in a toxic relationship. In his book, *Escaping Toxic Ties: Unraveling & Defeating Destructive Relationship Habits*, Dr. Dirk Stemper reminds us that toxic relationships aren't recognized through a positive diagnosis and, hence, are never recorded.[6] As a result, the lack of proper records limits what we know about the prevalence of toxic relationships. Yet he confirms that men and women are equally at risk of being trapped in an unhealthy relationship. A lot of what we know about the ripple effect toxic relationships have on mental and emotional health is gathered from the stories of friends, family members, coworkers, and acquaintants, sharing their relationship challenges and how they impact them. It is visible in real life and online, in the media, blogs, articles in glossy magazines, and online contributions. There is no denying it. We are often victims of the relationships we're in.

There are predominantly ***three ways*** in which exposure to a toxic relationship impacts your mental and emotional state. There is *a **growing sense of self-doubt** and **increased isolation***, while prolonged exposure to such a stressful environment, especially when you should feel safe within your romantic bond, leads to ***chronic stress***. As a result, toxic relationships serve as a cause for an increased risk of developing post-traumatic stress disorder (PTSD), anxiety disorders, depression, substance abuse, and an increased interest in suicide, leading to a rise in suicide attempts.

---

6   Stemper, D. (2023). *Escaping Toxic Ties*. Psychologie Halensee.

The dramatic impact of exposure to a toxic relationship has a mental and emotional strain rooted in human biology. The human brain's neural development centers around forming strong and healthy social bonds that enable us to connect with others and allow healthy and productive social interaction. Exposure to a toxic relationship, especially when this toxic state is present within your bond with your chosen romantic partner, disturbs the natural reward system associated with human interaction. Instead of experiencing an increased release of feel-good hormones, your body is exposed to a surge of stress hormones, like cortisol. Being in such a relationship automatically exposes you to high levels of stress for an extended period of time, which negatively affects every aspect of your well-being. Typically, exposure to chronic stress is referred to as a feeling of being stuck in a situation for which you see no way out. If you're already doubting your abilities and are feeling isolated, lacking access to a vital support system, it is even harder to escape this position.

As toxic relationships cause chronic stress, you can expect the decline in your mental and emotional state to impact your physical health in the following ways:

- Headaches occur more often and are more severe.
- Being sick more regularly or struggling to recover from ailments when too much cortisol has weakened your immune system, making you more susceptible to disease.
- Indigestion occurs as the digestive system slows down during high-stress states.
- Insomnia and restless nights cause a lack of sleep as stress exposure disturbs your sleep pattern. This leads to feeling fatigued, having a lack of focus, and being more irritable.
- Long-term exposure to elevated blood pressure due to an elevated cortisol level causes chest pains, heart palpitations, and other symptoms of a stressed heart and cardiovascular system.

- ✧ Stress also causes clenched jaws, teeth grinding, and many other unexplained muscle pains and stiffness.

While bad, these are symptoms that can still be largely reversed once you eliminate your exposure to stressful situations, people, or environments. However, if these symptoms go unchecked for too long, they can escalate into far more serious and often irreversible conditions.

When Your Relationship Is No Longer Serving You

Realizing you are in a toxic relationship can be the hardest thing to do. Initially, you may be doubting yourself, even blaming yourself for the problems in your relationship. Once you're convinced that it is indeed a toxic bond you're in, it is only human to enter a state of denial. Many find it too hard to admit they made a mistake when choosing their romantic partner. It may also be that you're embarrassed about the state of your relationship or are scared of what others will think when you acknowledge the state of your bond. It can be extremely challenging to reach out and ask for help when your relationship causes you to feel isolated. So, the sooner you recognize and acknowledge the concerns in your relationship, the sooner you can come to terms with what you're facing and take the necessary steps to protect your mental, emotional, and physical well-being.

As every relationship is unique and I have no prior knowledge of your romantic bond, I am refraining from providing a specific measure to determine the state of toxicity in your bond. However, allow the following questions to guide you in identifying the level of toxicity in your bond:

1. How does your partner treat you after you have an argument?
2. Is your partner open to talking about your concerns regarding your relationship? Do they acknowledge and respect your feelings and viewpoints, or do they dismiss your emotions as nothing?

3. Are you the one who is always sacrificing what is important to you for the relationship?
4. Does your partner apologize when they make a mistake?
5. How does your partner respond when you need to address work calls or texts after office hours?
6. How does your partner treat you when you're being vulnerable?
7. How do you approach difficult situations like a brewing argument?
8. Does your partner respect your relationship with other people?
9. How does your partner treat you in public?
10. How does your partner respond when you're enjoying success or have an achievement to celebrate?

No relationship is perfect, and it may be okay that some of the red flags of a typical toxic relationship are present in your relationship, but if you find several of these red flags or some of these concerns are causing a deep negative impact on your life, it is pretty evident what you're dealing with and why you need to set yourself free.

Chapter 5

Honoring Your Boundaries

Stop asking why they keep doing it and start asking why you keep allowing it.

—Unknown

Setting boundaries in your relationship is a sure way to reclaim your power over your life.

Imagine you have the most magnificent garden. Every morning, when you open the curtains in your bedroom, a vibrant sea of colors greets you. You're proud of your garden, and you should be, as it required a lot of work to create this breathtaking landscape. However, one morning, when you open your curtains, you immediately notice something is off. You can't really put your finger on what is wrong with your garden, but it is just not the same. The situation has you thinking for a while, but then you continue with life as usual.

The next morning, the situation is even worse. You immediately notice the footprints on your lawn, the broken branches in your hedge and your dahlias! Yesterday, the bushes were covered in huge, colorful heads, and now only a few of them are left hanging. Who could do such a thing? You struggle to get through your day. The invasion of your privacy and the disrespect shown to you and your garden fill your mind with negative feelings, leaving you feeling violated and helpless to stop the next attack on the beauty you've created. That night, you don't close an eye, and finally, before the break of dawn, you hear it. Voices in your garden. You rush to the window and while you can't make out the faces of the perpetrators, you now know that someone is coming into your garden and stealing your flowers.

While you don't mind sharing what is important to you, you want to do so on your terms. So, you build a fence to protect your garden. But because you don't want to keep everyone out, you install a gate. Now, you can control who has access to what you cherish and guide those whom you're willing to let into your garden, depending on when and where they're allowed to enter. Sure, some will protest, but they are the ones who didn't value what you had to offer in the first place. You reclaimed power and are now protecting what is important to you. You created a boundary— not to block all others out, but to apply control over whom you let in.

How Boundary-Setting Can Remedy Toxic Relationships

Relationship boundary-setting is no different. When there is no threat to what you value, the need to set boundaries will be minimal, if present at all. However, when your relationship is toxic, you can watch helplessly as your partner treats you in a way that disregards everything you value. Or you can set boundaries to shield yourself, your values and beliefs, your dreams and goals, your friendships, careers, identity, mental and emotional health, and your physical state from this onslaught.

Boundary-setting in any relationship, but even more so in one with a toxic nature, *is a way to reclaim yourself.* It is an empowering move to secure your safety.

It is also a way to maintain your identity. Do you remember those early days in your relationship when the love was so sweet, and your entire existence was soaked with infatuation? Being smitten is a dangerous place to be, especially for those who are somewhat insecure or very young. It is very simple to give up on yourself and allow your partner to suffocate you or absorb your entire identity into that of your relationship. In *Boundaries: Where You End and I Begin*, Anne Katherine shares how relationship boundary-setting is also a tool to establish and maintain your identity.[1]

Use your boundaries to eliminate toxicity from tainting your identity and losing yourself in a relationship bond.

Exploring the Challenges You May Face

Like erecting a fence around your garden will upset those who entered freely and took what they wanted from the beauty you created, setting boundaries in your toxic relationship will surely be met with resistance. By reclaiming your power, you're keeping your partner from abusing their power and getting what they want. Know that this resistance is to be expected, but through proper preparation, you can be ready for any attack your boundaries may have to endure.

This resistance can take the form of confrontations, with your boundaries deliberately tested to see if you're going to stick to the consequences you presented. You may find that your partner is overplaying their hand, blaming a lack of clarity on what your boundary entails. You may be rejected or face attempts to bring you public shame. Yet none of these challenges is as

---

1 Autor: Anne Katherine. (2000). *Boundaries : where you end and I begin*. Simon & Schuster.

devastating as giving up on yourself by not doing what you know is best for you.

The biggest obstacle keeping you from setting proper boundaries can be you. According to Brené Brown, self-love is a prerequisite for effective boundary-setting. She explains that boundary-setting demands that you love yourself enough to risk disappointing others in the process of doing what is right for you. It is a state you only enter once you no longer depend on external approval to value yourself. She says, "Only when we believe, deep down, that we are enough can we say, 'Enough!'"[2]

Do you value yourself enough to let go of the toxicity you're facing in your relationships?

Tips for Effective Boundary-Setting

Are you procrastinating setting essential boundaries in your romantic relationship because you're not sure where to start or how to do it effectively? It doesn't have to be that hard. Adding the following tips and strategies to your toolbox of emotional management skills will empower you to set the healthy boundaries needed to protect what is important to you.

- ❖ *An early start on boundary-setting will make life so much easier,* now and in the future. The longer you accept what is unacceptable, the more the unacceptable turns into the norm and the harder it becomes to change the norm to what you want it to be. So, the best time to implement boundaries in your relationship is right at the start.

- ❖ The first step is to *identify what type of boundary* will resolve the unpleasant experiences you have in your romantic bond. The *five most common types of boundaries* are emotional boundaries (protecting your

---

2   Brown, B. (n.d.). *Brené Brown: 3 Ways to set boundaries.* Oprah. https://www.oprah.com/spirit/how-to-set-boundaries-brene-browns-advice

emotional individuality by not assuming the mood of your partner for instance, when they're angry), intellectual boundaries (protecting your values and beliefs), physical boundaries (protecting your body), financial boundaries (protecting your money and financial health), and sexual boundaries (protecting the level of intimacy you're comfortable with).

- *Identify any potential violations,* as it is better to clear up any loopholes in your boundaries before expressing them than to change their wording afterward.
- *Determine the consequences* if your boundaries aren't respected.
- *Effective communication* is the cornerstone of successful boundary-setting. It means that you have to pick your timing to air your concerns, express your boundaries well, and clearly communicate your expectations to ensure you minimize resistance. As effective communication is the key to effective boundary-setting, this is the area where most of my tips center.

  - Describe the situation, stating what your expectations are and how not having them met is having a negative impact on you.
  - Use "I" statements as you want to refrain from coming across as attacking your partner.
  - Rely on a clear and concise manner to express what you expect and what the outcome will be if your boundaries are disregarded.
  - Clarify how your boundaries will benefit your relationship and perhaps even your partner to highlight how sticking to these boundaries is for the greater good of all.
  - Determine whether your partner grasps the importance of the matter, what your boundaries entail, and what you expect of them. It is also a good time to ask if they have any boundaries they would like to state.

- Remember to employ active listening skills to engage entirely in the conversation.

✧ Remember, *boundaries are tools to protect what you value,* not an aid to get back at your partner or an excuse to be resentful toward them.

Chapter 6

Embracing Grief and Loss and Moving On

*Like wildflowers, you must allow yourself to grow in
all the places people thought you never would.*

—E.V. Rogina

There is a massive difference between knowing that you're in a toxic relationship and that the longer you stay in this bond, the more it taints your soul, and breaking up, cutting yourself loose, and letting go. The latter can be unexpectedly hard, even if you knew it was the best thing to do or that there was no other option to resolve the matter and save your sanity. Mourning a lost relationship remains hard, even if it is a toxic one. For the longest time, you might have envisioned what freedom would feel like and perhaps even wished that day to come. But there is no way to prepare yourself entirely, as you will never truly know in advance what it will feel like once you're free.

Should that be a deterrent or an obstacle keeping you trapped? No! Have you ever heard the saying, "You shouldn't drink poison just because you're thirsty?" If not, print it out and place it in all high-traffic zones in your home, for just as you would never drink poison to quench your thirst, you should never reconnect with a toxic partner just because you're lonely.

A far more constructive approach would be to progress through the stages of mourning so that your mind, spirit, and body can recover from past wounds and flourish once again.

Why Feelings of Grief and Loss Follow a Breakup

Even if your partner caused you emotional pain, their place in your life will still leave an emptiness once the relationship ends. This emptiness can cause you to feel a sense of loss and demands that you progress through the stages of grief to heal. A breakup also constitutes a major change in your life; you're no longer part of something (the life of your partner and your relationship) larger than yourself.

We also need to consider the increased uncertainty that accompanies the end of a relationship. Likely, you envisioned your future with your partner, made plans that included them, and built around your situation while still in the relationship. As the relationship is no longer there, you're forced to return to the drawing board of your life and replan your future, and that can be daunting. Considering these factors, it should come as no surprise that a breakup can trigger a state of depression.

The Stages of Grief: A Rollercoaster of Emotions

Do you find yourself at the end of a relationship, unsure about the next direction your feet should take? Do you feel overwhelmed by the immense loss you're experiencing, often doubting whether ending your relationship was the right choice to make?

Allow me to offer some guidance: you will not progress until you progress through the four stages of grief. Only once you have experienced every stage and learned the lessons each stage contributes to your personal growth will you be able to progress through them all and experience complete healing.

The five stages of grief strongly remind us of the stages of forgiveness covered in Chapter Two.

- ❖ **Denial.** At first, you may deny that you're feeling a sense of loss. Your denial can also center on the belief that the relationship is over, as you may still be convinced that your partner is returning at some point. How long you spend in this stage and how often you return to it (since you can progress and regress between stages several times) will depend on you alone.

- ❖ **Anger.** A surge of negative emotions directed at your former partner is on the rise. There are so many reasons that can spark your anger. You may be angry at your ex for what they did to you, how much of your time they stole, the financial strain they left you in, the heartache, betrayal, rejection, or any other negative emotion or circumstance you need to face in their absence.

- ❖ **Bargaining.** Once the vigor of your anger subsides, you start to temporarily forget how bad your relationship was. You're keen to give it another go, and if that isn't an option, you're willing to just be friends (merely a smoke cloud to wedge your way into the same toxic situation again slowly). Don't do it. Persevere, for gradually, these emotions will subside, and the less time you stay fixated on them, the sooner they'll dissipate from your life.

- ❖ **Depression.** You've given up on restoring the relationship or revamping it as a friendship and come to realize you're entirely alone. Feeling so utterly alone triggers feelings of abandonment, rejection, and isolation. You may even convince yourself that you'll never be happy again and will die lonely one day.

- ❖ **Acceptance.** Then it happens, almost as if only once you accept that it is over and make peace with the idea that you're going to be alone, the serenity of acceptance brings steps in. Now, you can look back on your time of mourning and see how you've grown and how much better off your life is outside of the trap of relationship toxicity. As a result of learning from past mistakes and being optimistic about the future, you are now prepared to change your course.

Strategies to Process Grief Productively

Dr. Kim Maertz from the Mental Health Center of the University of Alabama has the following helpful strategies to process grief and move through it effectively:[1]

- *Acknowledge your feelings.* The harder you're trying to suppress emotions, the more pressing and prevalent they become. Emotions (much like people) want to be recognized and acknowledged. Rather, identify what you're feeling and call it what it is (even when you know these feelings, like jealousy, regret, or resentment, are not leaving you proud).

- *Take care of yourself.* It is very likely that the time you spent in the toxic relationship has been characterized by a lack of self-care, showing kindness to your mind, body, and soul, and refraining from doing the things you like. Every situation has pros and cons, and having the time to do all these things is surely a pro you shouldn't neglect noticing.

- *Let it go.* Much easier said than done, I know. But when I urge you to let it go, I mean actively reminding yourself that there were reasons why this relationship didn't work (very good ones, if I may say so). Stop agonizing over plans to get back together. I know it is hard, but this hardship is temporary, while losing yourself in a toxic relationship has the potential to impact your entire life.

- *Focus on the positive side.* Remember, we always get more of what we're focusing on. The more you're going to wallow in the past or how bad your current situation is, the worse it will get. Rather, list the pros of

---

1 Maertz, K. (n.d.). *Surviving a relationship break-up -Top 20 strategies.* https://www.mcgill.ca/counselling/files/counselling/surviving_a_break-up_-_20_strategies_0.pdf

single life. Focus on all the good things about being single and start making them part of your life.

- *Start dating again.* Just because this relationship didn't work out as planned doesn't mean that you're doomed to be alone for the rest of your life. Perhaps you've lost your trust in humanity and can't see how you'll ever be able to trust someone else. Start by trusting yourself. You've made mistakes, trusted the wrong person, learned from your mistakes, and can now progress wiser and with far greater discernment regarding whom you're willing to spend time with.

Will a closure ritual help you to shed the burden of grief and loss? It is an option Dr. Maertz suggests, but let's dig deeper to see why finding closure is so important.

Finding Closure and Letting Go

Closure is an essential step toward letting go of a relationship. The mere fact that you *have to let go* or *must find closure* is indicative that the relationship had a significant meaning to you. As a result, the need for closure differs from person to person and depends on how much you value what you've lost.

Ultimately, you're the only person who can truly say whether you need closure or not. But if you find it hard to move on with your life and are often regressing through the stages of grieving your failed relationship, it is best to take the necessary steps to find the closure you need to move on with your life. Closure brings about several benefits, but one huge risk is involved: you may not get the exact closure you visualized or thought you needed to move on. This is especially the case when finding closure depends largely on the actions, choices, and behavior of others.

Practical Steps to Finding Closure

What can you do? Identify the type of closure you want with the persistent awareness that it may not happen as you want it, but also while being open

The Simple Art of Letting Go

to the idea that you may just find closure through your actions, thoughts, and behavior. In simple terms, you may be looking for closure externally, and in your quest to find it, you may discover true closure was nestled inside of you the whole time.

To safeguard yourself against disappointment (while it is also a far more productive approach to look within), take control of your life and initiate the process needed to find the closure you seek.

- *Write a letter (and then destroy it).* Put your feelings into words. Unspoken words can gnaw away at your soul, and it is best to get the emotional weight off your chest. So, write that goodbye letter and be sure to say everything you want to do to free yourself from the burden you're carrying. Then, when all is said and done, burn the letter or shred it into pieces and step into your freedom.

- *Start keeping a journal.* A journal is another place where you can shed your emotions and unburden yourself without ever verbally expressing your feelings or thoughts, which you may later regret ever sharing with others. Journaling is also a good way to measure your progress. Noticing your progress is a good way to stay motivated and move forward.

- *Cry. Cry a lot, if necessary.* Sometimes, words are lacking to express feelings, and then tears offer a welcome release of the emotional charge disrupting your inner peace. So, embrace your tears. You may even have to find a quiet spot where you can have a good, undisrupted cry. Usually, except for a stuffy nose and red, swollen eyes, you'll walk away feeling much better about the situation.

- *Find a positive and uplifting distraction.* Are there any hobbies you have always wanted to pursue but never allowed yourself the time to do them? Now, your time is yours, and you're free to explore the world to your heart's desire. While getting involved in a new hobby will shift your focus away from the loss and heartache you may be feeling, it will also help you meet new people and form new bonds with those who have no knowledge of your former relationship.

- ✦ *Believe in yourself.* Sometimes, the hardest thing is to believe that you're strong enough to overcome obstacles such as loneliness, feelings of rejection, regret, disappointment, or failure. Always remind yourself of moments in the past when you did overcome hardships that may have had similar features. You're stronger than you may think, and if you struggle to remember this, be sure to phrase it into a positive affirmation to remind yourself of your potential every day.

Cultivating Self-Compassion

The belief that you're stronger and more capable than you may have first thought is balanced on the foundation of self-compassion. Showing yourself compassion and kindness is essential to letting go of a toxic relationship. Breaking up and amputating yourself from your toxic partner is the first step in the direction of showing yourself more compassion. Yet, it is a continuous process to enjoy persistent progress.

In the book *Rebuilding: When Your Relationship Ends*, authors Bruce Fisher and Roberto Alberti identify several essential building blocks to rebuilding your life after a breakup.[2] The foundational layer consists of bricks like denial, fear, adaptation, and loneliness, which are the first feelings you may experience. But as Fisher and Alberti continue to build their pyramid of blocks higher until they reach the peak of freedom, they explore building blocks like trust, love, purpose, and openness. These are the blocks necessary to rebuild your life, which you'll find through practicing self-compassion.

---

2   Fisher, B., Alberti, R. E., & Satir, V. (2012). *Rebuilding : when your relationship ends*. Impact Publishers.

The Role of Self-Compassion in Navigating Pain

Dr. Kristin Neff is a pioneer in the field of self-compassion, the author of numerous books on the topic, and the founder of Self-Compassion.org. She defines self-compassion as the process of turning compassion inward, displaying a similar level of kindness as you would toward others. It means that you choose to remain kind, caring, and understanding toward yourself and be patient instead of critical. The latter will only cause you to feel inadequate, like a failure, and prone to making mistakes.[3]

Her studies reveal that self-compassion is essential to improving and sustaining overall wellness. It increases resilience, supports coping mechanisms, enables you to achieve your goals, and leads to higher satisfaction and joy in life.

In the absence of self-compassion, the likelihood increases that you're berating instead of supporting yourself. Enduring an increased burden of criticism is demotivating and disempowering, leading to a propensity to give in to unproductive behavior and adopt unhealthy coping mechanisms that suppress instead of manage pain.

It's indeed a dire picture I am painting, so let's shift our focus to the positive side. Increased self-compassion *inspires greater motivation to adopt healthy coping mechanisms* as part of your healing journey. It *empowers you to persevere and show resilience* when facing painful emotions, circumstances, or any other form of trigger. Self-compassion *increases self-acceptance* and *awakens a greater sense of confidence* in your ability to overcome your challenges. It inspires *an increase in self-esteem,* improving your relationships while also helping you to *embrace your identity.*

Self-compassion is the foundation from which you can manage pain effectively.

---

3   Neff, K. (2015). *Self-compassion.* Self-Compassion. https://self-compassion.org/

Overcoming Critical Thoughts

Critical thought and persistent negativity in inner chatter are toxic to the mind and kryptonite to self-esteem. Such thoughts naturally result from exposure to the toxicity of your relationship. Hence, until you let go of your toxic relationship, new negative thoughts will continue to surface and rule your inner dialogue while crushing your self-esteem. Therefore, staying in such a bond is the complete opposite of self-kindness, an essential element of self-compassion.

Even worse, perhaps, is that there is often an unawareness of the negative mental chatter going on inside. An unawareness of the nature of our mental chatter is the Achilles heel for many struggling to let go of any negative experiences and the wounds they left.

As you can't change anything you're not aware of, the first step to silencing negative thinking is to become aware of what is taking place in your mind. This can be done by applying a greater sense of awareness to your inner dialogue. Mindfulness exercises, meditation, and journaling are all good ways to increase awareness of your thoughts.

Transforming Negative Thinking

Once you have identified the nature of your thoughts, you have to determine their origin and what serves as triggers to set off this kind of thinking. And then the real transformation starts, as there are several approaches you can apply to change the way you address yourself.

- *Change the language you use.* Take an example of a self-critical statement you often repeat. Are you criticizing the person or the action? For instance, saying, "I am so stupid," means something different than saying, "I am being so stupid." Semantics? Not at all. In the first statement, you're criticizing your entire being— who you are, what you stand for, your values, dreams, goals, everything! The second statement is different. While still critical, it only centers around a specific action or occasion. There is no intention to belittle the person, namely you. If you initially struggle to switch to being positive, aim to direct your criticism more directly, excluding who you are.

- *Start a self-criticism jar.* I am not sure how many households still have a swear jar or whether I am giving away my age by even mentioning it, but back when I was a kid, it worked quite well. Every time you swear, you would have to place a specific, predetermined amount of money into the swear jar. That sucked and served as an excellent deterrent to stop swearing and change your behavior. Use the same concept to punish self-critical thoughts. Determine an amount you have to put into the jar; whenever you find your mind murmuring critical thoughts, it's time to pay up. While this exercise increases awareness, it also encourages change in behavior.

- *Rephrase the negative into a positive.* If you're not initially comfortable enough to change your words and statements to reflect positivity, start by changing them to at least reflect a neutral perspective of yourself. From here, you can progress to making positive statements. When you become aware of a self-critical statement, pause it, test it to see if it is factual and if not, change it to state something positive about your identity. For instance, "I suck in the kitchen!" may appear to be a relevant statement if your meals are not as delectable as you wish them to be, but there are more positive ways to comment on your cooking skills. One way of doing this is by saying, "I am still learning a lot about cooking."

What self-critical phrases you often use need a similar make-over?

How will you rephrase these to give them a positive charge?

Turning Part Two into Practice

Are you ready to claim all of this and apply it to your life? Through this mindfulness exercise, immerse yourself in the warm comfort of self-compassion.

Self-Compassion Through Letter Writing

Letter writing may be a dying art, as we're a generation opting for far shorter forms of communication, but it remains an effective tool to confront and overcome negative emotions. It is also an amazing aid to encourage self-compassion as you'll see when following the next three steps.

- **Step 1:** Identify a feature, lacking skill, or trait that leaves you feeling inadequate. Explain in detail what it is, how it makes you feel, and how it impacts your life choices and behavior and, as a result, limits your future prospects. Only stop once you bring all the negativity out into the open and onto paper.

- **Step 2:** Now you step into the shoes of an imaginary friend. It is someone who cares deeply about your overall well-being, sees you for the amazing person you are, and is desperate to help you see yourself with the positivity you deserve. You, being your imaginary best friend, received the first letter from you and now need to reply in a truthful but also loving, kind, and supportive way. Write this letter to yourself.

- **Step 3:** Once Step 2 is complete, put down the letter and take a time out. Put some time and distance between yourself and the words on the paper before returning to reading your words. Notice the positive feelings it inspires. Do you find the letter soothing? Is there a spark of connection, love, and kindness toward yourself? Can you see what a powerful force of self-compassion can be? Make practicing self-compassion a part of your daily routine!

The most logical next step from the foundation of increasing self-compassion is to explore how you can silence your inner critic for good and let go of its power in your life. Meet me in Part Three for a final rendezvous with your inner critic.

Part 3

Your Inner Critic

Our biggest enemy, the most destructive force we have to conquer, is within. We may perceive external threats to our freedom as daunting, powerful, and wicked, but the greatest destruction causing an implosion of the self comes from within. It is called our inner critic, and while self-criticism can be noble, constructive, and supportive of personal growth, it can just as easily turn into the opposite, weakening your foundation until the implosion of the self occurs.

Are you ready to learn how self-criticism undermines your self-esteem and inner peace?

Let's dig in and explore strategies to cultivate self-compassion and quiet your inner critic.

Chapter 7

Understanding the Inner Critic

Self-criticism of the tired mind is suicide.

—Charles Horton Cooley

It was a Monday afternoon like any other... And then it wasn't anymore. What happened wasn't supposed to, and yet it did. Shortly after 2 pm, life changed forever for 62 people and their families affected by what happened. But it wasn't only their lives that were impacted; many witnesses, followers, and those calling the area home will always recall the event in varying degrees of vividness.

I am currently following the trial of events as they're released to the media about a collapsed construction site, trapping more than half of the construction workers on site. It was a mere few weeks before the building would've been completed and ready for residents to move into the apartment block, and then it gave in and collapsed on itself. It is an event that shook the community of the small town called George, located in South Africa.

The Simple Art of Letting Go

Disaster strikes daily around the globe, and I can't say for sure why this story stuck with me. Perhaps because the raw plight of a dad whose son was trapped was broadcast early on, sparking my empathy for all affected. Fortunately, when hope was beginning to dwindle, his son, trapped for almost two days on the second floor of a four-story building, surfaced from beneath what was now merely a heap of rubble, with only minor injuries.

Perhaps I am hooked on this story because it is so devastating, so sudden, and the entire event so awkward, as the nearly completed block simply collapsed into itself on a nice, sunny day.

Of course, there will be investigations to determine the cause of the collapse. This investigation will take months to complete, months of agony until those who suffered tragedy and trauma will finally be able to move closer to a place of closure. Nevertheless, there is already early speculation about what could have caused such an event. One such speculation is that buildings collapse into themselves without damaging the property surrounding them when they lack strength in their foundation. When there is weakness, it gradually deteriorates until it all gives in. This is called an implosion. By no means any less devastating than an explosion, you see.

I can't help but draw some parallels between this tragedy and how our inner critic, at times, becomes a weakness in our foundation. It initially may be nothing more than a point of strain, evolving into a hairline crack, gradually growing longer and wider. Then, perhaps on a bright and sunny day like no other, the foundation of our mental, physical, and emotional well-being can no longer carry our weight, and we collapse, trapping all that is important, meaningful, and close to us within. It's a tragedy! And like many other tragedies, this, too, can be prevented.

Seeking the Origins of the Inner Critic

I want to introduce you to a powerful force. A force that can impact every thought that comes to your mind. It will determine every action you take, your common behavior, and the words you speak. This force decides whom you'll be friends with and the nature of your relationships. It controls your journey to wealth, success, and contentment in life. It is a force so powerful that it can change the way you see the world. It can completely disempower you if you allow it to, if you succumb to it instead of controlling it, for ultimately, the creator of this force is you, your mind, to be more specific, and the neural pathways formed in your brain.

I am referring to the force of your inner thoughts, which can either be positive and uplifting and serve as your greatest supporter or be a destructive critic, demolishing any hope, dream, or sense of satisfaction in life you may have.

My reasoning behind calling you out as the creator of your own demise through persistent negative thought patterns isn't to upset you or to place the burden of your misery entirely on your shoulders. No, my intention is to wake you up to the realization that you have ultimate control and can reclaim your power once you understand how the inner critic originates. This knowledge can expand to teach you how to remedy your current situation and transform your inner voice into a positive force, taking you beyond the barriers you believe existed for you in life.

It's All About Neuroplasticity

Just in case the term neuroplasticity doesn't sound familiar; it refers to your brain's ability to constantly change and increase density in specific areas as neural pathways increase or become more prominent in certain areas. The brain is never in a stagnant state, as the impulses you're exposed to and the thoughts you entertain create neural connections. Every thought or impulse will either expand on an existing pathway or create a new path.

Thinking about neuroplasticity often triggers the following visualization for me: I see a luscious green lawn with a "Keep off the grass" sign posted to protect the greenery. Around the lawn are well-established pathways, and those who often pass the lawn adhere to the rules and stay on the pathways.

One night, a strong wind blows the sign away but for a few days, people still adhere to the rule and stick to the pathways.

Then, one day, a visitor arrives, unaware of the sign's existence and walks right across the lawn. The visitor stays for several weeks, making the same trip across the lawn daily. Others notice this changed behavior and also start to use the shorter path across the lawn. Gradually, a new pathway forms, quickly becoming the preferred path. It has become wider and is far more prominent now. As the former pathway is no longer used, it becomes less obvious and gradually starts to become covered in grass. If this process continues, the new pathway will become the only path, as the former will disappear entirely.

The same happens in your brain. Certain impulses will always result in specific thoughts unless you decide to force them in a different direction. The more you send impulses down this new pathway, the more you establish this new path, and as the former neural pathway is used less often, it gradually loses its prominence. This formation of new pathways in the brain is possible due to the brain's ability to change, an ability called neuroplasticity, which means that you can change the way you think about matters. *You can change your inner voice* from critic to campaigner!

One of the main obstacles to overcome in this quest is realizing your power, as the voice of your inner critic is so familiar. It is something that began to develop during your earliest childhood years. Every time someone makes a harsh remark criticizing you, the neural pathways your inner critic commutes on become more established. It's not just critical remarks we have to consider but also age. The prefrontal cortex, a part of the brain that doesn't fully develop until the age of 25, is extremely vulnerable to negative feedback throughout your entire childhood. Hence, negative feedback tends to have a more definite and longer-lasting impact when you're exposed to it at a younger age, as you simply lack the emotional intelligence to process any kind of comment or feedback accurately.

As you internalize these comments or external feedback, your brain perceives this input as critical of the self and forms pathways to accommodate critical feedback. These changes primarily affect the prefrontal cortex in the brain. Additionally, because it is a component of the brain that doesn't fully develop until the age of 25, your brain is extremely vulnerable to negative feedback throughout your entire childhood, which makes these pathways more noticeable.

As a result, you're likely to be more critically inclined toward yourself. Such a critical perspective results in limited beliefs about what you're capable of, self-doubt, lowered self-esteem, anxiety, and depression. These outcomes can have a lasting impact into adulthood unless you make a conscious decision to take control over your inner voice, allowing you to change its tone.

Quantifying the Impact of Self-Criticism

It is widely understood that the voice of the inner critic has a detrimental impact on mental health and well-being. Some common assumptions are that it leads to an increased risk of depression and anxiety. It can also evolve into far more serious mental health concerns like psychosis, generalized anxiety disorder, obsessive-compulsive disorder, and social anxiety disorder. Even if your inner critic hasn't yet had such a negative effect on your mental health, it's still likely that you experience feelings of helplessness, being trapped, being stuck in your life and circumstances, or lacking motivation to move forward.

Sadly, these aren't mere assumptions, as various studies have proven them. A paper published in the June 2018 edition of Science Direct confirms the detrimental impact your inner critic has on your mental health and refers to numerous study results backing these unfortunate findings. Under the lead of Ruth McIntyre of the Institute of Psychiatry, Psychology, and Neuroscience at King's College in London, the group determined that self-criticism (judging and scrutinizing yourself harshly and punitively) leads to self-defeating behavior. It results in a decline in the number of interpersonal goals you have, and it is at the root of a depressive personality style. They also confirmed the link between inner criticism and social anxieties, PTSD, and eating disorders. The list of confirmed concerns associated with an active inner critic is lengthy, turning your inner critic into possibly the most powerful internal cause of self-sabotage, to the point of self-destruction.[1]

However, you don't have to feel helpless in the face of it all. You can disarm your inner critic!

Disarming the Inner Critic

Our Freudian heritage includes psychoanalytic theory, offering a greater understanding of the interaction between three distinct agents of our psyche's structure: id, ego, and superego. Many perceive the latter as a pseudonym for the inner critic. The superego is the gatekeeper of morality, the one persistently keeping the desires of the ego in control, often through a critical approach or through rewards for positive behavior aligned with societal values and expectations.

Initially, the superego doesn't sound so bad at all. But, according to Freud, an overactive superego leads to neurosis as it causes the ego to battle for control, resulting in the loss of psychic energy and maladaptive behavior.[2] As this is a futile attempt to bring the superego back into line or silence the inner critic, we must explore more productive means to disarm the inner critic and reclaim control.

Identify the Three Cs in Your Self-Talk

Only through greater awareness can you acknowledge the destructive force coming from within. Hence, the first step is to be mindful of your inner

---

1   McIntyre, R., Smith, P., & Rimes, K. A. (2018). The role of self-criticism in common mental health difficulties in students: A systematic review of prospective studies. *Mental Health & Prevention*, *10*, 13–27. https://doi.org/10.1016/j.mhp.2018.02.003

2   Mcleod, S. (2024, January 25). *Freud's theory of personality: Id, ego, and superego*. Simply Psychology. https://www.simplypsychology.org/psyche.html

dialogue so that you can record what it is saying. Journaling is a wonderful tool to compile such a record, enabling you to notice patterns and identify specific triggers.

Once you have established such a record, explore the nature of what is being said. These are usually one of the following three Cs: comparison, criticism, or complaints.

- Are you *comparing* your entire life with certain aspects of those of others and persistently falling short?
- Are you *criticizing* yourself and using harsh words to diminish your self-worth?
- Are you trapped in a perspective where only the hardships of your life can be seen, and you're incapable of taking a step in any direction away from the position of *complaining*?

Identify Your Type of Poison

Self-criticism isn't a one-size-fits-all concern. There are different types of self-criticism, and understanding which category your inner critic falls into will guide you in reclaiming your power.

- *Catastrophizing.* Do you often exaggerate matters or expect the worst to happen?
- *Personalizing.* Do you perceive everything wrong to be your fault?
- *Filtering.* Do your mental filters only allow the negative to enter your mental space?
- *Overgeneralization.* Does one bad event or failure convince you that you're never up to anything good?
- *Mind reading.* Do you believe you know what others think and that it is never good for you?

- *Polarizing.* Do you see the world in black and white, leave no room for error, and disregard any leniency based on circumstances?
- *Emotional thinking.* Do you confuse feelings and thoughts, often thinking something must be true just because you feel a certain way?
- *Should statements.* How often do you make statements like 'I should do better', 'should know more', 'should've understood', or 'should've done something'?

Isn't the last type especially extremely disempowering? How is there any escape from what you should've done when it is always uttered in retrospect?

In Chapter Two, we covered *mindfulness exercises,* and in Chapter Six, we explored *self-compassion* and how to *practice self-kindness*. Revert to these, as they're both wonderful aids in dethroning the superego.

Another simple but powerful approach is to *practice gratitude* by making it a daily habit to express all the things you're grateful for.

Regular practice of *positive affirmations* is another antidote to the ever-pessimistic inner critic. If the conscious mind chooses to be positive, the inner critic cannot spread its toxic criticism in the subconscious. Drafting effective positive affirmations becomes even easier and more effective once you identify the exact nature of the tone your inner critic uses. For instance, if you are constantly receiving overgeneralized criticism, a simple affirmation like, "I am resourceful and capable," may be the best remedy.

These are all effective tools to have in your tool kit to protect your mental health against the onslaughts of your inner critic.

Chapter 8
Cultivating Self-Compassion

Unlike self-criticism, which asks if you're good enough, self-compassion asks, what's good for you?

—Kristin Neff

We're all programmed to be negative. This phenomenon is called the *negativity bias,* and it simply means that, in general, we all tend to see the glass as half empty rather than half full. In general, we tend to see the worst possible outcomes first, notice the cons of every situation, and give preference to the negatives in our minds.

Being biased in this manner isn't at all a bad thing. It is what makes us more alert in threatening situations. Quite simply, negativity bias contributes to the survival of humankind as it makes us more alert and better prepared for any challenge or threat. It has been the case for as long as we've existed. Centuries ago, threats presented themselves as the saber tooth keen on catching the prehistoric hunter, and today, these threats can present themselves as bad business deals. Thanks to the negativity bias, we are better prepared to manage either situation.

However, when the negativity bias becomes overactive, you are in a difficult situation that calls for greater resilience to overcome obstacles. Do you find yourself in a situation that calls for self-compassion because it will give you the resilience to overcome the challenge that the voice of the inner critic presents?

Connecting Self-Compassion and Emotional Resilience

Emotional resilience is essential to overcoming hardships and facing stressful situations, and it is also the foundation needed to cultivate a growth mindset. A growth mindset demands the persistent desire to know more, expand your knowledge and skills, and better yourself. It is essential to be able to allow yourself to make mistakes and, when you do, dust yourself off and try again. The latter demands a high level of resilience, advancing resilience into not merely a nice-to-have feature but a characteristic essential for success in life.

While some people are naturally more resilient than others, emotional resilience is, fortunately, a skill that can be developed and strengthened. Practicing self-compassion is one such tool to bulk up your emotional resilience, but how does it work?

Like the inner critic, emotional resilience is mostly shaped during childhood years. Growing up in an environment that radiates safety while feeling understood and accepted offers the most favorable conditions for emotional resilience to develop and flourish. Yet, if you missed out on this, a situation mostly beyond your control, it's good to know that it isn't too late for you! By shifting your perspective and changing your choices, you can cultivate all the emotional resilience needed to overcome the challenges in your way.

Effectively, what you want to do is expand your *window of tolerance*. Window of tolerance is the term used to refer to your ability to respond swiftly and effectively in stressful situations. The wider your window of tolerance is, the greater the stress intensity you'll be able to resist. A narrow window of tolerance translates to being easily triggered and becoming anxious, stressed out, or panicky in the presence of stress. So, the smaller the window, the less stress you can manage, and the wider your window, the more stress you can resist.

Four significant factors impact the amount of stress the window of tolerance can handle.

- First, we have *adverse childhood experiences and past trauma*, which cause the window to shrink. However, by applying the strategies presented in Part One, you can counter this effect and increase your resistance to stress.
- The second factor is *trauma at a later stage in life*. Here, too, we have already discussed several solutions, like practicing mindfulness and self-compassion.
- *Chronic stress* is another influential factor to consider. Prolonged exposure to a high-stress state has such an immense negative impact on your mental, emotional, and physical well-being that it is impossible to maintain a healthy window of tolerance, making you less resilient.
- Finally, we have to consider the detrimental impact of the absence of proper self-care on your tolerance window. Just consider how much harder it is to get through a stressful day after a night of disrupted sleep. Or how easy it is to become anxious over even insignificant matters when you're not feeling well.

So, let's apply a little reverse psychology here: if the absence of self-care narrows the window of tolerance, then practicing regular and meaningful self-care and self-compassion will widen the window, making you more resilient to face challenging situations.

While self-compassion is essential to emotional resilience, it is not where its benefits end. The advanced benefits of self-compassion are best explained by Emma Seppälä, Ph.D, the science director of the Stanford Center for Compassion and Altruism Research and Education. "With self-compassion, you value yourself not because you've judged yourself positively and others negatively but because you're intrinsically deserving of care and concern like everyone else. Where self-esteem leaves us powerless and distraught, self-compassion is at the heart of empowerment, learning, and inner strength." [1]

Cultivating the Components of Self-Compassion

Self-compassion is undeniably essential to ensuring a strong foundation and preventing the implosion of identity and existence. From the extensive writings of Dr. Kristen Neff, a pioneering researcher, teacher, and author on the topic of self-compassion at the University of Texas, we learn that self-compassion consists of three components. These are self-kindness, humanity, and mindfulness.

- *Self-kindness stands in opposition to self-judgment.* Dr. Neff explains that self-kindness equates to being understanding of oneself in times of hardship, challenge, or failure. That means it's all about being gentle with yourself when things don't go as planned. Life doesn't always go the way we want it to, and we don't always get what we want or perhaps think we deserve. However, when self-kindness is practiced instead of self-judgment, you gain greater resilience to pursue your goals and continue your efforts.

- *Humanity is the counter to isolation.* It is so easy to think you're alone when you face hardships. The isolation resulting from this way of thinking takes you to a lonely place, making it much harder to show resilience. A much better approach is to perceive whatever battle, hardship, or setback you're facing as part of human nature. We all suffer in the same manner, even though the conditions of our suffering may differ. You can lessen the hurt that isolation brings and find it easier to persevere by seeing your difficulties or suffering as a part of a larger suffering that everyone experiences.

- *Mindfulness is preferred over over-identification.* This point is closely linked to the previous, as once you can see your hardship as part of the greater human suffering, your perspective on the matter changes, allowing

---

1 Hart, H. (2019, September 3). *How self-compassion can help you cope with adversity: 3 Steps to improve your resilience.* Forbes. https://www.forbes.com/sites/hannahart/2019/09/03/how-self-compassion-can-help-you-cope-with-adversity-3-steps-to-improve-your-resilience/?sh=5d42ae87825f

you to be more mindful of your feelings, acknowledging their existence instead of judging or suppressing them for they may not fit into what you consider acceptable. Simultaneously, mindfulness also prevents you from overidentifying with your feelings. An example of over-identification is when you consider yourself a failure instead of merely judging your attempts or actions as failed.

Are you keen to know how you can apply these three components of self-compassion in life to strengthen your resilience? Let's assume the difficult situation you're facing is that you lost your job through a major retrenchment caused by a dire global economic state. This situation is extremely stressful, and your inner critic is at it, relentlessly whispering harsh remarks in your ear, placing immense pressure on your foundation.

- **Step 1:** Take a step back to observe your situation. You might want to say, "I'm having a hard time right now," "I'm going through a difficult time," or "My circumstances are seriously challenging me." Express your observations. These statements all serve to acknowledge what you feel, but refrain from inflicting any negativity on your identity.

- **Step 2:** Now, you can apply common humanity as you recognize the challenge or hardship you face to be something many others are also battling with in life. You may not be the only person at your company who has been laid off. Unemployment is on the rise in many industries, leaving families without an income. Regardless of your situation, it is important to see the problem you're facing not as a your problem but an *us* problem, with us being all humankind.

- **Step 3:** Now, you can apply self-kindness. Instead of beating yourself up with statements like, "I should've worked harder," or "I am such a failure, nobody is going to employ me," or even "I am failing my family," opt for words of kindness, the type of words you would offer to a friend in a similar situation. Speak words of positivity unto yourself, like saying, "What can I do for me?" or "I wish myself well."

A grounding technique you can use with this exercise to emphasize the positive impact it will have is placing your hand on your chest to offer comfort when you make these positive statements.

How will these statements help me get a job? How will self-kindness and compassion pay my rent at the end of the month? These are all questions I expect you to ask. And I have a counter question: How does allowing your inner critic to blast you with harsh and critical feedback help you achieve the necessary improvements to your current state or situation in life?

Honestly, neither of these types of statements will pay your rent, get you hired, or secure a much-needed interview. Yet, while your inner critic is leaving you feeling depleted, emotionally drained, and ready to give up, self-compassion provides motivation, inspiration, encouragement, and trust that all will improve eventually, and so it expands your window of tolerance by increasing your resilience.

Celebrating Your Imperfections

The legend has it that the 16th-century monk, Sen no Rikyū, was eager to learn all there is to know about the important and still existing Japanese ritual of a tea ceremony. To expand his knowledge and understanding, he visited the tea master, Takeno Jōō. The latter was a wise man and wanted to test Rikyu's capabilities before agreeing to teach the aspiring apprentice. So, he asked him to clean his garden. Rikyu worked hard in the garden and was eager to impress the tea master, so he cleaned it up from top to bottom. Once he was done, he shook the cherry tree to let the Sakura flowers fall to the ground before calling the garden master to inspect his work. This moment of the imperfect beauty of flowers on the ground in a well-cared-for garden is widely understood as the birth of the concept of *wabi-sabi*.[2]

Rustic is likely the most accurate English word to translate the Japanese concept of wabi-sabi, yet it still doesn't convey the meaning of the practice

---

2   Walther, A. (2021, January 8). *What is wabi sabi? The elusive beauty of imperfection*. Japan Objects. https://japanobjects.com/features/wabi-sabi

and principle entirely. Andrew Juniper, author of *Wabi Sabi: The Japanese Art of Impermanence*, defines the term as follows: "an intuitive appreciation of ephemeral beauty in the physical world that reflects the irreversible flow of life in the spiritual world." Furthermore, he links the origins of wabi-sabi, a Zen idea, to a history of Taoism as he takes his readers through the patchy history of the development of the concept of wabi-sabi, today understood as finding beauty in simplicity and imperfection.[3]

Directly translated, *wabi* is associated with a disconnection from the vanity of materialism to free the mind to indulge in spiritual abundance, while *sabi* is linked to the passing of time and the natural state of impermanence in the cosmos. You can revert to Chapter Three to read up more about impermanence and how to use this natural state of all existence as an aid in letting go.

I encourage you to embark on an independent journey of exploration of wabi-sabi, but for our purpose, it will suffice to understand that wabi-sabi serves as a reminder that all things are impermanent, incomplete, and imperfect. And so are you. It encourages us to seek beauty in the simpler, imperfect things in life. The cracked teapot, the chipped artwork, the scratched painting, and the imperfect you are all mesmerizingly magnificent and beautiful.

You don't have to be a Zen Buddhist to practice wabi-sabi. Today, even modern psychology recognizes the benefits nestled in the search for imperfection and the appreciation of the beauty it holds. Seeking and celebrating these imperfections in yourself is a sure way to silence the harsh, critical voice of your superego and inner critic and devalue your self-worth.

Once again, I have to admit that celebrating your imperfections won't resolve your shortcomings in life. But hey, neither does the persistent torrent of criticism coming from your superego aid in improving yourself. However, once you allow yourself to accept and appreciate your imperfections, you will experience a deep-rooted and immensely impactful transformation.

---

3   Juniper, A. (2003). *Wabi sabi : the Japanese art of impermanence*. Tuttle Pub.

This transformation will empower you to live larger, with more gratitude, confidence, and appreciation, enabling you to achieve so much more.

- *Seek to see the beauty in your imperfections.* Are you painfully aware of all that is wrong with who you are? Great! Now, explore how these imperfections make a positive contribution to your life and the greater world you belong to. Reflect on your flaws with the intention of seeing how they contribute to your unique character and expressing your appreciation for how they set you apart.
- *Use your imperfections and flaws to connect with others.* One certainty is that we are all flawed. By celebrating our flaws, it is easier to connect with other flawed people, shedding the sense of isolation the inner critic bestows upon us for not being perfect.
- *Focus on the progress and experiences along your journey instead of the desire for perfection.* Find beauty every day, make magnificent memories, and use every moment to enjoy life and enrich your existence, as then every moment becomes meaningful.
- *Seek ways to utilize your imperfections to benefit others.* Once you can turn your imperfections into useful tools to contribute to the lives of others, flaws increase in meaning. How can you use your flaws to better the lives of others? Perhaps acknowledging your flaws and allowing yourself to be vulnerable by confidently sharing your imperfections with others encourages them to do the same.
- *Surround yourself with like-minded people.* When you're around people who are striving for perfection, it becomes much more difficult to accept and celebrate your flaws. Choose your crowd well and so gain the support needed to succeed in this quest.

Allow a deeper understanding and appreciation of your imperfections to support and strengthen your foundation, making you more resilient to face the emotional burdens of life.

Chapter 9

Challenging Negative Self-Talk

Everything you tell yourself matters. It will either lift you up or tear you down. It's your voice and your choice.

—Kara Lambert

So, up to now, a lot has been said about negative self-talk and how your superego or inner critic will persistently drown you in an influx of harsh and mean criticism if you don't put a stop to it. But how bad is it really? Let's look at the stats.

According to the National Science Foundation, we're thinking between 12,000 and 16,000 thoughts daily. Of these thousands of thoughts, 80% are classified as negative. While this is bad, we haven't touched on the worst yet. The foundation also determined that 90% of our thoughts are repetitive. It boils down to us thinking the same negative thoughts over and over until we start to believe and become what we think we are.[1]

---

1   Vaugh Clark, J. (2023, January 12). *How negative self-talk is affecting your goals*. LinkedIn. https://www.linkedin.com/pulse/how-negative-self-talk-affecting-your-goals-jeremy-clark-mba/

These statistics lead to the reasonable assumption that if you're going to think you're not good enough and those thoughts find a footing in your mental cycle of repetitive thoughts, you'll become not good enough. If you think you're not smart enough, you'll never reach beyond your self-imposed limitations. If you think you'll never succeed in life, find love, lose weight, or become healthy, then you are effectively laying the groundwork for your thoughts to become your reality! What you think matters. Buddha said, "What you think, you become. What you feel, you attract. What you imagine, you create," and science proved it to be true.

How Negative Self-Talk Suffocates Self-Esteem

In Chapter Seven, we uncovered several severe and highly disturbing consequences of persistent exposure to the voice of the inner critic. I am specifically referring to the increased risk of severe mental health concerns linked to excessive rumination. Yet, the negative impact of negative self-talk is suffocating your self-esteem, restricting your brilliance, and robbing you of joy and contentment in life long before any mental health diagnosis.

- *Cramping your creativity.* Negative thinking results in limited thinking. As you tend to see the cup half empty rather than half full, every creative thought is short-lived as the mind instantly shifts focus to fixate on impossibility. The longer you remain fixated on how it can't be done, the less likely you'll be to come up with creative solutions to turn your visions into reality.

- *Always falling short.* Life demands that we challenge ourselves. Success, whether it is in love, business, or life, often expects us to place ourselves out there and step into vulnerability with bravery. But how long will you continue to do this if you're constantly reminding yourself of your imperfections? For how long will you be willing to risk it all in search of what you're looking for if you persistently believe you're not good enough to get it, experience it, or achieve it? Eventually, there is no better prospect than not even trying.

- *Becoming needy.* For as long as you struggle to accept yourself, you'll persistently seek validation and acceptance from others. Then, you hand over your power and step into neediness, always begging, seeking, and canvassing for acceptance. Such a level of neediness is toxic to your relationships, compromising the strength of these bonds and eventually causing them to crumble.

- *Depression sets in.* Initially, it may not be depression you're battling; it is just a deep sense of lacking satisfaction and disillusionment in life. However, gradually, the shadow of failure and fault encumbers you and depression becomes inevitable.

Negative self-talk starts robbing you of life long before mental health concerns step in.

Using CBT to Reframe Negative Thinking

There is a lot we can draw from cognitive behavioral therapy (CBT), which serves as a helpful aid and strategy to silence the inner critic and transform your negative thinking into positive inner chatter.

In *The Negative Thoughts Workbook*, Dr. David A. Clark advises us to *know our traps*.[2] When he uses the word 'traps', he's referring to the memories we persistently ponder and allow to repeat in our minds. This kind of rumination is not only futile but also highly toxic to your entire being and threatens the state of your existence. He refers to these thoughts as repetitive negative thoughts, or RNT, and states that these thoughts can center on any incident, setback, or disappointment in life. While it is fine to have negative thoughts about these events, as it is only human to feel and think this way, they do become toxic when you allow them to linger for too long in your mind.

For a thought to be classified as an RNT, it has to be *repetitive, negative, intrusive,* and *unshakable,* meaning you find it hard to transition away from

---

2   Clark, D. A. (2020). *The Negative Thoughts Workbook*. New Harbinger Publications.

the specific way of thinking. Furthermore, RNTs are also *uncontrollable,* as you may not yet have identified specific triggers instigating the departure of the toxic mental journey. They are *abstract,* as while they inspire stress and anxiety, there is very little if anything, you can practically do to prevent the dreaded outcome you are persistently pondering. Lastly, they're *passive,* and you're left at the mercy of factors and people seemingly beyond your control.

Dr. Clark continues to explain how these characteristics also form a cycle of thinking, with one leading to the other. However, he also offers the following steps as part of a CBT strategy to break free from this chain of thinking. So, let's jump right in to break free from the grip your inner critic has on your life and mind.

- List three events or life experiences you're regularly thinking of.
- For each of these events or experiences, identify their negative aspects and expand on how and why they lead to increased stress.
- Next, you need to test them to see if they are repetitive, negative, intrusive, unshakable, uncontrollable, abstract, and passive.

Put all concerning repetitive thoughts through this evaluation process, and once you're done, you'll have a complete list of thoughts to assess.

- Now, *challenge each thought individually* by asking whether it is true. Test it against facts and evidence to clarify if this thought is based merely on a belief (which is mostly the case when it comes to negative thinking) or factual.
- As these thoughts are merely based on beliefs, you can *start to push back by questioning their validity,* presenting counter arguments, and replacing the statements made in a kinder tone.
- Gradually, as you ease into the process of transforming the tone of your self-talk, you'll gain the necessary confidence to erase them entirely and *replace them with positive statements.* Now, you'll be able to compile statements to express youth thoughts with self-compassion, and so

expand your resilience, instead of slapping yourself down with harsh and unfounded criticism.

Mindfulness Techniques to Quit Flying on Negative Autopilot

How often do hours pass without you even noticing? Or perhaps moments of shifting to autopilot occur more often when you're driving a familiar route, and miles go by without you noticing the changing surroundings? Moments of drifting off can even happen in conversations. These are moments when we're operating on autopilot, floating on a cloud of unawareness of our environment, feelings, actions, and yes, thoughts.

Being in autopilot mode means the subconscious mind is minding the store. If the inner critic is determining subconscious thinking, you're placing yourself in a vulnerable position, pleading for a state of mindfulness to break the toxic chain of thinking.

Mindfulness is what brings you back to the present and empowers you to stop ruminating. It encourages acceptance, love, compassion, and kindness. It also increases vigilance in responding to negative feelings as soon as they enter your mind. Mindfulness allows you to direct your attention to where it serves you well, increases awareness of your current state, and allows you to engage, confront, and stop negative thinking.

Throughout the book, we've explored several mindfulness exercises that encourage a general state of increased mindfulness. In Chapter One, we explored various helpful *breathing techniques* to assist in this regard. It is also where we looked at *various ways to be more mindful* while busy with our daily activities.

Meditation, especially the observer meditation explored in Chapter Two, is extremely helpful to increase active thinking and awareness and put a stop to negative thought patterns.

Now, I want to share another mindfulness exercise that will help elevate an overall sense of mindfulness and so, limit time spent on autopilot as an aid to reduce the airtime you give to your inner critic.

Mindful Yoga

Mindfulness and yoga have always gone hand-in-hand, as the ancient practice strengthens the mind-body connection as it relies on *asana* (body posture) to increase a state of mindful awareness. The practice also encourages a state of observation of sensations and experiences, both internally and externally, without judging them or reacting upon awareness.

I'll be the first to encourage you to take mindful yoga seriously, and I suggest enrolling in a class taught by a qualified yoga instructor. However, four yoga poses are specifically helpful for increasing mindfulness: Tadasana, Vrikshasana, Anjaneyasana, and Supta Baddha Konasana.

Tadasana

Another familiar term for Tadasana is the Mountain Pose. It is a simple pose to practice at home, but it does require some commitment to keep your mind from wandering.

1. Stand tall with your arms next to your sides.
2. Distribute your weight evenly across the entirety of your sole to have a firm stance.
3. Keep your pelvis in a level position, front-to-back and side-to-side.
4. Extend your spine to grow taller, lifting your chest while keeping your lower ribs from moving out of alignment.
5. Relax your shoulders down the back to open your heart.
6. Keep your ears centered over your shoulders and your chin parallel to the floor.
7. Maintain your position for as long as it's comfortable while breathing deeply in persistent awareness of how the flow of air makes you feel.

Vrikshasana

The Tree Pose aids in increasing focus and mindfulness as it requires you to maintain your balance on one leg. While it can be easy to wander off, losing your balance will quickly bring you back to the present moment.

1. Stand tall with your arms next to your sides.
2. Shift your weight to the right foot.
3. Inhale while lifting your left foot from the floor and rotating it to the outside.
4. Place the sole of your left foot on your right thigh.
5. Bring your hands to your chest, palms together for the prayer position.
6. Ensure that your left foot is pressing firmly on the right thigh and your right foot remains firmly, with an equal weight distribution, on the floor.
7. Stay in position for as long as possible while continuously breathing deeply.
8. Once done, shift to the other side.

Anjaneyasana

The Low Lunge is not only good for improving balance and core strength, but also for inspiring a greater sense of mindfulness.

1. Start in the Downward Dog position, bending forward and forming a triangle between your feet, arms, and the floor.
2. Take a step forward with your right foot and place it next to your right thumb so that your right knee and ankle are aligned.
3. Bring your left knee to the ground behind your hips.
4. Lift your torso and raise your arms above your head.
5. Your biceps should be next to your ears and your palms should face each other.

6. Move your hips slightly forward until you feel your left leg stretching in front.

7. Pull your coccyx to the floor using your core muscles.

8. Pull backward with your thumbs, while shifting your gaze upward and bending your back only slightly backward.

9. Hold your position for as long as possible while remaining mindful of every awareness in your body and mind.

Supta Baddha Konasana

The classic pose often used at the end of a yoga session is also known as the Reclining Bound Angle Pose. It is the ideal pose to raise inner awareness.

1. Start in the Corpse Pose, laying on your back with arms somewhat away from your body and feet about hip-width apart.

2. Bring your soles together while allowing your knees to fall open.

3. Visualize your groin area sinking into your pelvis, pressing firmly on the floor.

4. Spread out your arms 45 degrees from your sides with your palms facing upwards.

5. Relax from the top down. First, allow your face to get into a resting state.

6. Then progress to your shoulders, chest, abdomen, hips, knees, and feet until you're entirely relaxed and dropped down onto the floor.

7. Maintain the position for as long as it is comfortable while staying in a state of awareness of every sensation.

Practice a series of these moves for several minutes per day and notice how much less intrusive your inner critic becomes.

Part Three in a Nutshell

The foundation on which you build your entire life is laid during childhood when you have little to no control over what is happening to and around you. It is also a time when neurological development hasn't occurred to allow you to process feedback, comments, and how others treat you in an emotionally mature manner. Hence, this foundation is easily weakened or flawed, causing it to be insufficient in strength and endurance to carry the burden of adult life.

Yet, unlike a foundation set in concrete, you can improve on the strength of your foundation, making it more resilient to carry the load your life expects it to bear. By silencing your inner critic, you can grow stronger from your roots upward. By changing the tone of your internal narrative, you can increase your resilience. And, by embracing a positive outlook on who you are and showing yourself compassion, you can endure much more while also deriving greater joy from life!

Part 4

Your Identity

Who are you when you're stripped naked of all material possessions and status quo? Or when you're not attached to any social circle or title? When you're not defined by social expectations?

When you stand barren and there is nothing but you, what is the true nature of your identity? What do you base this definition of yourself on? And even more important, is this image portraying an authentic version of you?

Identity is a tricky concept. It is a version of ourselves that we create and try our darndest to maintain all our lives, as we believe it is more acceptable to the world than who we really are. This can easily become a quest we're so engaged in that we forget who we really are and simply adopt this false persona, which we've been creating for so long, as our own.

Sticking the incorrect label on anything is a dangerous quest. We put a lot of pressure on ourselves to live up to expectations that we can't meet, which strains our relationships. I'm not even going to mention the tremendous internal stress it causes— the mental and emotional conflict of leading a life that we created but isn't in line with our nature. This is a false identity, the overexaggerated persona you imitate, a unique kind of toxin you need to let go of to set yourself free.

Chapter 10

Exploring Self-Identity

Life isn't about finding yourself. Life is about creating yourself.

—George Bernard Shaw

"You see, I was a creative master of classroom incidents. One of my favorite activities was doing obscene birdcalls in class. I would get away with talking like a sailor because I did it like I was imitating a bird, so you had to listen carefully to hear that I was actually saying something dirty or making fun of the teacher. The teacher, of course, was usually trying to ignore me, leaving her no time to interpret my calls, so I had a field day, making some of the students around me grab their sides in laughter." In *Have a New You by Friday,* Dr. Kevin Leman continues to share more of his classroom antics and how he became a master artist of classroom performances, like carving a hole in a book through which he could shoot at his fellow students with a water pistol without them knowing where it came from or setting the garbage bin on fire to get out of a test.

His performances continued to grow bolder and more daring, consuming his mind as he had to maintain his position in the spotlight as the classroom performance artist. That was until one day in April 1961 when his math teacher, Miss Wilson, sat him down and said, "You know, it occurred to me the other day, and I wonder if it ever occurred to you that maybe you could use some of the energy you expend on these antics to really make something of yourself rather than just being the proverbial class clown— at your expense, I would add."[1]

Considering that Dr. Leman became an internationally known psychologist, speaker, and author of multiple books, he took Miss Wilson's words to heart at the age of 17 and did make something of himself. His immense sense of humor and entertaining style, which are also characteristics of his reputation, never left him; however, rather than using his sense of humor as the foundation for his true identity, he used it as a building block.

Who would you be if you weren't so busy being someone you're not? Growing into the person you're meant to be also means letting go of the identity —the persona you've been so busy creating— but before we get to that, let's first delve deep into the nature of self-identity, exploring what it is and what it's not.

Analyzing the Multifaceted Nature of Identity

The trusted *Merriam-Webster* dictionary defines identity as "the distinguishing character or personality of an individual."[2] Oh boy, how I wish it were as easy as that, for what we're about to uncover about the true meaning of identity leaves us with a far more complex conundrum. But understanding identity in all its complexity also opens doors, enabling you to seek, find, and celebrate your true identity.

---

1 Leman, K. (2011). *Have a new you by Friday: how to accept yourself, boost your confidence, & change your life in 5 days*. Revell.

2 Merriam-Webster. (2018). *Definition of Identity*. Merriam-Webster. https://www.merriam-webster.com/dictionary/identity

A first attempt to pin down a definition of identity would be to call it an amalgamation of all experiences, memories, relationships, beliefs, and values used to create an idea of the self. Daily, you add new experiences and memories to the amalgamation, causing it to change. By nature, identity is then a fluid concept, always evolving, mostly at a slow and consistent pace, but there can also be life-altering events resulting in a major shift in identity taking place, kind of in the wink of an eye.

Identity Is Our Experiences

Based on this definition of the nature of identity, it is easy to see why identity is often a matter of mere perception and that it lacks consistency by definition. Feelings, memories, experiences, perceptions, and observations can't be quantified and are unique to each and every one of us. There is no right or wrong way for how any event makes you feel, and not only do we all hold the potential to perceive and experience the same things in vastly different manners, but also newer experiences will change the manner in which you perceive past experiences, creating a gradual shift in your identity.

Identify Is Shaped by Physical Appearance

While a large component of your identity is based on feelings and perceptions, values, and beliefs, we can't deny that physical appearance, gender, race, socio-economic status, and religion are all contributing factors to how you define yourself. Your physical appearance may be the clearest and most consistent component of your identity. However, it is not entirely static, as variations in how a specific element of your identity is perceived will depend on your environment and those around you.

For instance, being Hispanic and living and working in a predominantly Hispanic community will highlight different aspects of a Hispanic identity than when living and working in a predominantly non-Hispanic environment. The same is true regarding religion, financial status, gender, and appearance.

Identity Is How We Think Others See Us

Identity is often perceived to be the answer to the question, 'Who am I?' Yet, it is far more often based on how we think others perceive us, meaning it is quite common to shape your identity according to how you think others see you rather than who you truly are. In this case, it is common to expand your identity based on the feedback you get from others or, let me say, how you perceive it. For instance, in Dr. Leman's case, his humorous antics in class became more elaborate, expanding his identity as the class clown because he perceived the laughter of his fellow students as positive and encouraging. However, from Miss Wilson's perspective, she could acknowledge that his actions and the feedback he was getting were at his expense.

The term identity is multifaceted, making it much trickier to define it accurately. Of course, the latter is essential to letting go of any false perceptions about who you are so that you can be fully and authentically you.

This brings us to the next important question: How is identity shaped?

How Is Identity Shaped?

Knowing how your existing version of what you perceive to be your identity was formed may reveal several pitfalls, revealing a misperception of who you truly are. Understanding how your identity is shaped can also guide you to the necessary steps to bring your identity into alignment with reality and to find and embrace your true self.

Family, friends, experiences (especially those occurring during childhood), culture, and location are some of the most prominent external factors shaping your identity. Internal factors with a contributing role are self-expression, personality, values, and beliefs. However, more important to consider are the three key processes or tasks identified in psychology as essential to shaping your identity. While following these three tasks isn't an entirely waterproof solution, it offers a structure for delivering an identity far more accurate version of your true self. The three tasks I am referring to are:

- Acknowledging and developing your potential
- Identifying your purpose in life
- Seeking opportunities to practice your potential and manifest your purpose

That said, even when following these steps, identity maintains its fluid nature since as you age and become more mature, your potential changes and increases while evolving maturity can change your life purpose.

How Societal Norms and Cultural Expectations Shape Self-Perception

If we compare forming our identity to creating a musical masterpiece, then society is our soundboard, and what it echoes back is often not so true, helpful, or kind. But the opposite can also be true. According to Tasha Eurich, author of *Insight: Why We're Not as Self-Aware as We Think and How Seeing Ourselves Clearly Helps Us Succeed at Work and in Life*, we can't trust the feedback of others, as people in general prefer telling *pretty little lies*.

She explains that often, instead of stating how we really feel, we choose to remain silent or to give only positive feedback instead of offering helpful truths that can guide us to better ourselves. It is not something we do on purpose. Tasha explains that it is an inherent feature of humankind. One can even say it is a survival skill; for as long as humankind has been around, it has been better not to bump over the apple cart containing social order and security. So, we say nice things that we don't mean, as speaking our truth might leave us feeling vulnerable.[3]

For as long as the soundboard to our symphony echoes back in a positively tainted version of our compilation of notes, it is impossible to understand the

---

3   Eurich, T. (2016, September 4). *Why no one is telling you the truth at work (and what to do about it)*. LinkedIn. https://www.linkedin.com/pulse/why-one-telling-you-truth-work-what-do-dr-tasha-eurich/

authentic nature of your behavior or how you can improve. Do you prefer living in this state of blissful ignorance? It sure may be easier to stomach, but will it make your life easier in the long run?

Meet Sara. She is 16 years old. Her best friend asked her to enroll in the school's talent competition. Initially, Sara declined, but later on agreed to do so. Why? One night, she was singing in the shower, and her mom made a comment about her singing. Her mum was distracted and didn't really give much thought to what she said to her daughter, but instinctively knew it had to be something nice. Sara took the compliment, and the next day, she enrolled to sing at the talent competition.

A few days before the event, she gave a trial performance to some of her best friends. They did what great friends do and supported her with a wave of positive feedback. So, it was no surprise that Sara was oozing confidence as an up-and-coming singer when she stepped onto the stage. Her confidence cup was overflowing with positive feedback, compliments, and admiration. While only a few days ago, she didn't even want to be part of the competition, she now sees her future as America's latest musical genius. Again, why? Because all the positive feedback she has been getting from her soundboard has changed her identity.

Sara's new identity wasn't authentic. Being a singer was only something she thought she wanted because those who cared about her the most chose to tell her the pretty little lies they thought she wanted to hear. The judges didn't agree, and Sara crashed and burned on stage. And what did her friends do? They told her she sounded amazing, was supposed to win, and that the competition was unfair.

Can you see how we tell each other lies, which effectively distort the image we have of ourselves to such an extent that it is entirely removed from reality?

Practices for Cultivating Self-Awareness

Fortunately, Tasha Eurich also provides us with three helpful solutions you can apply once you're mindful of the existing discrepancies in the feedback you get.

Seek Out the Indirect Clues

It is easy for us to taint our words, but it is much harder to taint our actions. Sure, you can ask for feedback, but don't take what is being said to heart. Rather, become mindful of the nonverbal feedback others give. Look for clues of authenticity in tone, gestures, facial expression, body language, and nonverbal sounds, as these are the elements of communication where we find it much harder to conceal the truth.

Be Discerning When Choosing Your Critics

Tasha references Professor John Jacob Zucker Gardiner's explanation of the three kinds of people who will surround you and immensely impact your identity. They are the *Unloving Critics* who will have nothing good to say (even if there is plenty to mention). The second category is *Uncritical Lovers,* who are really just giving you what they think you want to hear. While their intentions are good, their inability to stick to the truth doesn't serve your attempts to better yourself at all. Lastly, the most sought-after category is called *Loving Critics*. You can rely on them for the ugly truth— not because they're mean, but because they want to see you succeed and better yourself. They will give you compliments when compliments are due, but with as much ease, they will tell you with absolute honesty when there is room for improvement. They are the ones you need to choose to have in your life. Can you identify the loving critics in your life? Appreciate them when you do, for they're committed to your personal growth and who will help you shape your authentic identity.[3]

Listen, Then Respond

Even if the painful truth comes from a *Loving Critic*, it still remains painful. It can be so easy to check out of the conversation, decline the words of advice and wisdom, or disregard what has been said. But listen and do so well, and through listening, you can learn. Ultimately, learning is what sets you free from the stronghold an inauthentic identity will have on you, allowing you to embrace your authenticity!

Chapter 11
Embracing Authenticity

Authenticity is the daily practice of letting go of who we think we're supposed to be and embracing who we are.

—Brené Brown

I was sipping on a cappuccino, a cup of aromatic indulgence, in my favorite coffee shop. While taking a break from my book to take in my immediate environment, the ongoing conversation between two ladies at the table behind me fell on my ears. I only caught what seemed to be the tail-end of a juicy story about someone's boyfriend turning out to be someone completely different from who everybody thought he was. It was a conversation brought to a conclusion with the oh-so-popular phrase, "It's so hard to trust anybody nowadays!"

Are you familiar with that statement? Do you struggle to put your trust in anything or anyone, as the world so often presents us with mere reflections of what others want us to see, bombarding us with images that hide reality from the naked eye?

How much easier would life be if we were all just honest and truthful with each other? What would life be like if there were no mind games, manipulation, or blatant lies?

That world can exist, but to be part of the solution, we first need to stop being part of the problem. And being inauthentic about who you are equates to being part of the problem.

The Importance of Embracing Authenticity

Whether you're deliberately keeping up a façade or simply unaware of the false persona you hang onto, at some point, you need to ask yourself how much longer you can deny yourself the benefits stemming from authenticity.

1. *Trust.* One of the most important benefits of being authentic is making it easier for others to trust you. Regardless of how good you think you are at hiding your real persona, it is most likely the case that others will sense something is off. Sometimes, it is hard to pinpoint exactly what it is about someone else that makes you feel uncomfortable, but it often becomes evident if you pretend to be someone you're not. Just like you need to search for honest feedback in the nonverbal cues of conversation, you, too, will most likely fail to keep up appearances in the nonverbal elements of conversation. Discrepancies between what you say and these nonverbal elements kill trust; once trust is lost, it is almost impossible to reestablish it.

2. *A confidence booster.* Nobody can be a better version of you than you, which might be a bit of a cliché, and yet we so often find it so hard to wrap our heads around the truth it holds. There is literally nobody in the world who can do you better than you! All our lives, we strive to be the best at something, and when we find that one thing we're really good at, our confidence levels spike. That one thing can be just being authentically you. Try it and see how your confidence surges.

3. *Freedom!* The sought-after state of freedom is sought after by many and yet so easy to find. You don't have to remain a hostage to other's

opinions and perceptions, nor do you have to dance to someone else's tunes. However, nobody can grant you the freedom you desire except you. By embracing authenticity, you break the chains of all expectations, opinions, and assumptions. You become truly free to spread your wings and pursue greatness.

4. *Values.* Knowing your values is one thing; living according to them can be an entirely different quest. While having values and not living them is utterly useless and a complete waste of time, many find it important to live according to what they believe to be important. Your values play an important role in shaping your identity, and not living according to them creates internal conflict, causing immense stress and exhausting emotional strain. All of these hardships can be avoided once you embrace authenticity and your true identity.

Values and identity go hand-in-hand, as your values shape your identity, and staying authentic to your identity means you live truly according to your values. Living according to your values offers guidance toward setting and achieving your long-term goals; it offers you a sense of purpose, reduces stress, and improves your decision-making skills. Furthermore, honoring your values also serves as a boost of confidence and increases your resilience.

Confronting the Fear of Judgment

Early on in *The First Rule of Mastery: Stop Worrying About What People Think of You*, author Michael Gervais introduces his readers to the concept of FOPO, or the Fear of People's Opinions, by sharing the story of Lauren Regula. He shares the story of how the softball star was presented with a chance to play for Team Canada at the globe's most prestigious stage, the 2020 Olympics. There was just one snag: she retired 11 years ago.[1]

---

1   Gervais, M. (2023). *The First Rule of Mastery*. Harvard Business Press.

He continues to share her history with the Olympics and how a heartbreaking loss meant she came in fourth in the 2008 Olympics and just missed the bronze medal. So many might have considered the opportunity to get a second chance at that medal as the opportunity of a lifetime. Second chances don't often cross our paths. But that wasn't the case for Lauren Regula when the Canadian coach called her up to get her to join the team.

She hesitated. She wanted to do it, but she had serious reservations. Some were understandable, as making this commitment would mean being away from her kids for a long time to practice and then leaving for the Olympics. But these were concerns she could overcome with sufficient arrangements and calling in her support network to help with her kids. The concern pressing the young mother's mind was what people would think if she returned to the game to represent Canada. Would they judge her for leaving her young family? Would they see her abandoning her husband for her personal ideals? Her fear of people's opinions was standing between her and a chance to realize her dream. To complete the story of Lauren Regula, Canada won the bronze medal that year, and Lauren Regula was part of the team. She realized a dream, but if she had given in to her FOPO, that would have been something she would have regretted for the rest of her life.

Her story isn't much different from that of many others who live life according to other people's expectations, conform to their norms, and disregard our directives on what we want for ourselves and expect from life.

Gervais refers to this phenomenon as the setting of an invisible limit keeping us from fulfilling our purpose, which is the hidden epidemic.

FOPO, or the more psychologically correct term, the fear of negative evaluation, can hamper your performance and lead to self-defeating behavior. Eventually, it will crush your confidence and self-esteem, creating a mentally and emotionally toxic state. To address this concern, we need to understand why it exists.

A Need for Survival

Once more, we can relate the origins of the need to receive favorable judgment from your peers to a safety mechanism ensuring your survival. While it is still often the case in boardrooms and business networks that you have to ensure others like you to secure survival in a highly competitive market, the same truth is relevant in every other area of life, dating back (again) for as long as humankind has been around. The better you're liked, the greater the odds of having others backing you up, and the more secure you are in the world.

So you do what is necessary to save yourself. You say things you don't mean, agree to do things you don't want to and show a keen interest in matters that don't concern you. You betray yourself to ensure you make it another day. But is that really the case? Does survival depend purely on getting great feedback and avoiding judgment at all costs? And what is the price you pay in return?

Measuring Your FOPO

Thanks to the research of David Watson and Ronald Friend, we can measure to what extent this level of fear exists within you. They developed the Fear of Negative Evaluation (FNE) Scale to determine to what extent the fear of judgment is impacting your life. Mark Leafy, a professor of psychology and neuroscience at Duke University, reduced this rather lengthy test in 1983.[2] The abridged version of the FNE test contains only 12 questions, which I share at the end of Part 4.

Jumping the Barriers That Keep Authenticity at Bay

It's time to let go of what you believe to be a better version of you and to revel in your authentic identity!

But where do you start?

---

2   Rose, H. (n.d.). *Fear of judgement: why we are afraid of being judged*. Ness Labs. https://nesslabs.com/fear-of-judgement

- Identify and acknowledge your strengths. List the things you do that leave you feeling energized and excited. We all have things we need to do that will drain us. But there can be a long list of things you can do that will energize you, often even things that would drain many others. More often than not, you're also really good at doing these things. You can claim them as your strengths.

- Know your influencing factors. There are external and internal factors influencing the growth of your identity. You may be able to change some of these, but even if you can't, it is better to know what these things are and plan around them than to be blindsided.

- Know your values. The more you think about your values and look at them discerningly, the more accurately they will represent your identity. By exposing yourself to your values more often, you're also increasing your commitment to them and, similarly, your odds of staying true to them.

- Be mindful of your feelings. Revert to the mindfulness exercises shared in Chapter One. Following these strategies will increase your awareness of your feelings and help you notice any changes. These changes will indicate whether you're embracing or betraying your authenticity.

- Break down your big fears into smaller fears and challenges to overcome. By breaking down your fears into smaller steps, you can build up the courage to face those things you're most scared of doing— the things you steer away from and, in the process, cause you to fail to embrace your authenticity. Bravery doesn't have to be big. You just need to start somewhere and keep on going.

- Choose to be authentic daily. Even if it is only one small thing you do daily to embrace your authentic identity, do so. The more you practice this with the small stuff, the easier it becomes to tackle the bigger matters.

Reflect regularly on your level of authenticity and notice how it improves your life!

Chapter 12

Letting Go of Labels

I'm not an optimist. I'm a realist. And my reality is that we live in a multifaceted, multicultural world. And maybe once we stop labeling ourselves, then maybe everyone else will.

—Octavia Spencer

Stereotyping refers to the process of generalization, assuming that all members of a certain group share the same features. This generalization is often based on race, culture, age, gender, financial status, location, or religion. While there is a place for this type of generalization or labeling (for instance, in psychology to help build case studies or to identify various outliers from the norm), it can also be immensely harmful. Labeling becomes especially toxic when no room is left for individual differences within the group, making it a double-edged sword.

Why Is Labeling So Limiting?

Let me set the stage. It is a national game and a major sporting event. It can be basically any team sport played on a national level. The crowd has filled the stadium. Thousands of supporters are dressed in the colors of their team. Their faces are adorned with face paint. They resemble warriors from times gone by. They are ready, and they stand in unity, as they're all here to support the team they believe to be the best. Would you ask them if they are opposed to being referred to as supporters of a specific team? No way! They love the idea of being part of something larger than themselves. They want to be labeled as supporters of a specific team. And it is a perfectly normal phenomenon, for we find meaning and a sense of belonging when we can associate ourselves with something bigger than us. For some, this bigger thing is a sport; others find deeper meaning through association through religion or culture. There is nothing wrong with being labeled if it is a label you want to have.

However, the labels attached to our identity, the ones we don't want or like, are an entirely different story. These labels limit our potential. They attach traits to our identity that we don't like or feel simply don't fit. They rob you of your identity, are limiting, and are toxic.

These labels are also often linked to societal expectations— expectations you may not want to live up to but feel you have no other choice.

The Liberating Power of Letting Go of Societal Expectations

Whose songs are you dancing to?

Living your life based on the expectations of others is a frustrating and very limiting experience. If so, you find yourself in a toxic situation, imposing several challenges and restraints on your life.

One of the three most prominent challenges you'll face as long as you're living according to the expectations of others is that *you'll never learn what is good for you*. For as long as the primary goal of everything you do is to please someone else, your goals, dreams, and ideals will remain unfulfilled. What worsens the situation is that *you'll never be able to meet their expectations,* for what they expect of you is based on their perception of what you're capable of and how they see you. This is a viewpoint defined by their skills, values, beliefs, and life experiences. In fact, it doesn't have much to do with you at all. Hence, until you decide to let go of the desire to live up to these expectations, you'll remain trapped in a toxic place.

As external expectations aren't created according to your unique skill set, they're often *unrealistic or unreasonable*. Perhaps even both.

It may also be that what others expect of you and what you need to do to meet these expectations can contradict what you need to do to achieve your own expectations of yourself. So, essentially, your commitment to meet someone else's expectations is bound to *hinder or slow down* your progress toward pleasing yourself.

That's not where it ends. Planning your life according to what others expect of you can be detrimental on even more levels of life.

Living according to labels impacts your emotional well-being, as it often results in *frustration, disappointment, or even anger*. Your stress levels are bound to increase, which will eventually have a negative impact on your mental and physical wellness, too.

If practice makes perfect (and we know it does), then in the absence of practice, your skills will remain limited, to say the least. This is especially true when it comes to decision-making. When you make decisions based solely on what other people want for or from you, you never have the opportunity to make your own decisions. It means *your ability to make smart choices remains hampered*, affecting every area of your life.

Without the freedom to choose, *your opinion won't carry much weight either*. It leads to a *loss of respect from others and yourself*. Lacking self-respect contributes to *shrinking self-esteem* and a *decline in confidence*.

The Simple Art of Letting Go

Yet, while all these things happen and you're gradually becoming more painfully aware of how it impacts your life, your *inner conflict is on the rise*. And that is where *mental health concerns become a reality*. It is all just one whirlpool of toxicity slowly sucking you in until you press the button to eject from this poisonous situation until you decide to let go.

But how?

Ejecting From the Toxic Whirlpool of Expectations

It may feel like you're drawing, like you can't find your footing as the negative motion swirling you around helplessly is just too much; but there is hope, and it can be found in the following four steps.

- *It's their problem, not yours.* If someone has certain expectations of you and you fail to meet them, it is their problem, not yours. Your responsibility is solely to meet your own expectations in life.

- *Connect with your inner voice.* Is your inner voice nothing but a faint whisper? In Chapter Seven, we had several hearty conversations about your inner voice and how to turn your inner critic into one that adds positivity to your life. The insights shared there will help you turn up the volume of your inner voice, getting it loud enough that it can no longer be ignored. Only then will you be able to clearly distinguish between what you want and what others tell you to do.

- *Speak up.* You have a responsibility to use your inner voice and express what it says. Remember, only you can hear this internal chatter, and therefore, you are responsible for asking for what it needs and stating what you want.

- *Question motives.* Are you one of those people who agrees to every request or demand? I still have yet to come across a people-pleaser who doesn't believe that sacrificing their own needs, dreams, goals, desires, and wants will make them accepted and loved. It's a myth. While you may stay committed to this toxic behavior, honestly believing that doing so will positively impact your social status, it has quite the opposite effect. People struggle to respect those who agree with everything. Even worse is that you'll find many who are all too eager to abuse your need to please others, using you at your expense. A far more constructive approach is to question people's motives. It is perfectly fair to ask why they want you to do something or why they can't do it themselves. Be discerning about what you agree to do.

While these steps offer a helpful foundation to break free from the expectations others harbor of you, there is one more source of toxic expectations you need to break free from. What makes this an even more challenging quest is that these expectations come from within. I am referring to the unreasonable and unfair expectations you have of yourself.

Breaking Free from Self-Expectations

As harsh and unreasonable as the expectations others may have for you can be, the ones you may have of yourself are sometimes just bad.

- Are your self-expectations leaving you feeling like a failure?
- Are you setting the bar for yourself too high?
- Do you expect perfection in yourself and never seem to achieve it?

Unreasonable self-expectations with which you set yourself up for failure are disheartening, frustrating, soul-crushing, and destructive to your confidence and self-esteem. They inspire procrastination, lead to self-sabotaging behavior, cause frustration, and hamper your creativity. Simply put, they're a toxic part of your identity— a part you need to let go of to set yourself free.

- What opportunities have you missed out on because of your self-expectations?
- What is the true price you're paying for staying trapped in this toxic state?

- ❖ How much longer can you endure exposure to these unhealthy expectations?

Are you ready to let these unfair self-expectations go?

- ❖ *Be honest about your capabilities.* Part of embracing authenticity is being honest with yourself regarding your capabilities. I am all for lofty goals, but by setting unachievable goals for yourself, you're only setting yourself up for failure. How many failures can you endure before you're no longer interested in even trying? Rather, be more realistic by setting smaller goals that gradually build up to the greater goals you want to achieve.
- ❖ *Prioritize yourself.* What you think of yourself is of far greater importance than anybody else's perspective of you. Hence, only set expectations for yourself that are aligned with what you want for yourself and your future and that will help you achieve your goals.
- ❖ *Acknowledge and celebrate your achievement*s, even the little ones. These mini-celebrations will keep you motivated to achieve expectations and help you stay committed to achieving what you've set out to do.
- ❖ *You're not alone.* Remember when we explored humanity as a pillar of self-compassion in Chapter Eight? Don't isolate yourself on the quest to meet your self-expectations, as many others face similar challenges. By connecting with them, you can empower each other and be stronger in your quest.
- ❖ *Take the good with the bad.* Some days are good, others aren't. It is pretty normal to have ups and downs on every journey. Accept them both as part of your quest instead of allowing the bad days to dishearten you on your way.

Applying Mindfulness to Soar Above Labels

Whether you want to escape the burden of the bias of others or the heavy self-expectations you carry, mindfulness practices can bring some relief and pave the way to ultimate freedom.

Some more practical mindfulness exercises include being mindful about how you consume media or interact online. Both present a high risk of exposure to content that may impact the expectations you have of yourself or how you think the world perceives you, which translates into what you believe others expect of you. For instance, visualize yourself having a lazy Saturday. By late morning, you're sipping on your third cup of coffee, still in your pajamas, and your hair is a mess. You're mindlessly scrolling through posts on your social media pages.

Do you see posts of your online friends sitting in their PJs, too? No! People post only the best side of their lives on social media. So, you see posts of people dressed up, looking their best, and living the life you only dream of. How do they do it? Why are their lives so great when here you sit like a slob? Perhaps it's because you're not doing enough. Perhaps you're not meeting the necessary expectations. Did you just manifest the perception of what the world perceives as success, joy, and the ultimate life, coupled with the expectations you need to meet to make it happen for you? Can you see where I am going and how unfair expectations are created, even if only in our minds?

The best way to avoid developing the need to meet such toxic expectations is to be discerning with what you expose yourself to.

Loving Kindness Meditation

Instead of losing valuable time admiring the lives of others, try a positive mindfulness exercise to embrace your authentic identity and love yourself for who you truly are.

1. Find a quiet spot where you can sit undisturbed.
2. Sit down in a comfortable position and close your eyes.
3. Think of several phrases you can use to wish wellness upon others and yourself.
4. Breathe deeply a few times, and as you feel yourself immersing yourself in a sense of deep relaxation, use these phrases to express goodness to yourself by repeating them out loud.
5. Now, allow your mind to find someone else to whom you want to extend kindness. Preferably, this should be someone who is kind to you.
6. Think about what good wishes, like kindness, peace, love, and health, you want to extend to them, and express these wishes you have for them. For instance, "I wish X unconditional love."
7. Next, you can expand your circle of well-wishing by including people you're feeling rather neutral toward. Perhaps the receptionist at work or the guy from the copy room at your office. Wish them well in a similar manner.
8. Make the circle of loving kindness even wider and consider sending well wishes to someone with whom you have a strained relationship. Do you have a coworker with whom you just don't see eye-to-eye, or perhaps it is a family member with whom you can't get along? Send them well wishes.
9. Finally, include the entire universe and send well wishes to nature or abstract things, showing your appreciation for them, for being able to experience them, and for their beauty and magnificence.
10. Notice the increased level of warmth, kindness, and acceptance you feel within. Enjoy the moment before returning to your normal routine.

Make the loving-kindness meditation part of your daily routine to help you find peace within while letting go of the toxicity of holding onto matters that aren't part of your authentic identity.

Test Your FOPO

Now that you have a better understanding of the immense impact the fear of judgment can have on your life, I encourage you to use the following questions derived from Mark Leary's Brief NFE to guide you in thinking about how it affects your life.

1. Do you worry about what others think, even if it doesn't make a difference?
2. Does it make you worry if you know people are forming a bad impression of you?
3. Are you constantly scared that others will notice your shortcomings?
4. Do you worry that others will disapprove of you?
5. Does it bother you what others think of you?
6. Do you get distracted thinking about what others think of you while in conversation with them?
7. Does it negatively impact you if you know others are judging you?
8. Do you often worry that you'll do something wrong?
9. How often do you think that you worry too much about what others think of you?
10. Do you often worry about the impression you're making?
11. Are you scared that others will find fault with you?
12. How much do the opinions of others bother you?

Also, consider how much better your life can be if you let go of the need to betray your identity and start embracing authenticity.[1]

---

1 Leary, M. R. (1983). *A brief version of the fear and negative evaluation scale*. Personality and Social Psychology Bulletin 9, 371-376. https://www.div12.org/wp-content/uploads/2014/09/Brief-Fear-of-Negative-Evaluation-Scale.pdf

Part 5

Beyond Control

We build our lives around what we believe to be true and certain. Our dreams are founded on these perceived certainties. Similarly, these convictions also form the foundation for our goals while guiding every decision we make along the way. But what if what we believe to be certain just isn't? What if it is a mere illusion of reality, something we foolishly hold onto because the idea that we're in control offers a false sense of comfort?

Are you ready to take a step back from your life to enable you to look at it from a fresh perspective? Compile a list of things you believe to be certain in your life that you believe you have a degree of control over but, in reality, don't. Don't worry; if you're honest about the reality of these matters, it won't take long to list as few as 10 things from the top of your head. Let me help you.

How can you be absolutely sure that when you get into your car to commute to work, you'll arrive there safely? Or that you'll wake up in the morning when you go to bed? How sure are you that your job is secure and that you have financial certainty to care for yourself and your family? What about your health? Even people who are fit and eat healthily get sick. What makes you so confident in your health?

Merely thinking about these questions is anxiety-provoking, I know. I am not trying here to spike your stress levels or send you tumbling into anxiety, but I am touching on several common triggers keeping many awake at night, as it is often in the darkness that our truth and honesty steps rise to the surface on a wave of anxiety and stress. In the next couple of chapters, we're exploring how you can let go of these perceived certainties in life that offer a false sense of safety and why it is best to let this way of thinking slide so that you can let go of yet another burden pulling you down in life.

Chapter 13

Surrendering to Uncertainty

In detachment lies the wisdom of uncertainty...in the wisdom of uncertainty lies the freedom from our past and from the known, which is the prison of past conditioning. And in our willingness to step into the unknown, the field of all possibilities, we surrender ourselves to the creative mind that orchestrates the dance of the universe.

—Deepak Chopra

"This year is going to be amazing!" Shelly said these words so often every single day since the 1st of January that by the 10th, it became her personal mantra for the year. And she had plenty of reasons to believe this to be true. After some financial hardship and struggles to find a work contract that offered a decent salary, she was finally settled with an amazing company. She was passionate about her career, had an amazing home, and loved her life.

Sure, on the health side, she could be doing slightly better as she has been struggling to get rid of a cough for a couple of months already, but her doctor doesn't seem too concerned. At worst, this might only be chronic bronchitis she needs to gain control over. Hence, when she was sent for more tests, she truly didn't perceive the situation as a cause for concern.

Then the call came. "The doctor wants to see you. Can you come right now?'

'That sounds alarming.' Her mind stepped into a slight anxiety, but this, too, was something she could dismiss quickly until she couldn't do so anymore.

"I am sorry. You have lung cancer. It's stage 4. You need to get immediate treatment, as without it, you have about 3–12 weeks to live."

There is simply no way to quantify the level of stress and anxiety such a diagnosis brings. The carpet was pulled right from beneath her feet, causing her to tumble, gasping for air. How? Why? What? No!

Life sucks at times. It surely does. Especially when you've been holding on so tightly to what you believed to be true, only to hear that it is a mere illusion. Whether it is your health, career, marriage, being with a loved one, a child, financial certainty, or living in freedom and peace, there is no certainty in life that these things you hold onto will remain there forever. Not because you didn't hold onto these things firmly enough or treasure and nurture them sufficiently, but because the only certainty in having these things is the here and now. There is no way to predict what will happen a year, a week, a day, or even an hour from now.

Don't get me wrong. There is nothing wrong with planning your life based on your current circumstances, but leaning too heavily on these matters makes it even harder to recover once they're no more. So, how do you let go of your controlling need to squeeze them into permanence? Let's explore why it's so essential that you hold only tight enough so that you can let go with greater ease and comfort when and if life demands you to do so.

The Futility of Seeking Control Over External Circumstances

Before exploring why holding onto perceived control over external matters is futile, I want to soften the blow by stating the following: Absolute certainty isn't what we believe it to be. For the longest time, I also considered having certainty over certain important matters affecting my life a good thing. Until I endured the humiliation of being wrong about what I believed, advocated, and fought for to the extent that I pushed certain people out of my life.

Certainty Can Be Evil

During the 1990s, Dr. Roy Baumeister researched the concept of evil to determine what drives people to commit heinous deeds. He wanted to test the general assumption that people do bad things because they feel bad about themselves and that by causing others to feel bad, they feel better. Wrong! And this isn't my conclusion but, indeed, what Dr. Baumeister determined. He found that the worst criminals in the world were very proud of their deeds and had absolute conviction that what they did was right. Despite what reality portrayed around them, they believed with absolute certainty that their actions were justified. He determined they had unwavering certainty in what they perceived to be right.

For the majority of us forming the wider population, our absolute certainty doesn't cause us to break the law, but at times, it can result in our behavior being immensely hurtful to others and, even more frequently, us being wrong. In the New York Bestseller, *The Subtle Art of Not Giving A F*ck,* Mark Manson explains it as follows: "The problem here is that not only is certainty unattainable, but the pursuit often breeds more (and worse) insecurity."[1]

What is the alternative, according to Manson? He states, "the more you embrace being uncertain and not knowing, the more comfortable you will feel in knowing what you don't know."

That is the paradox of uncertainty, confirming that certainty is far more emotional than rational. It is the persistent search for something that will ensure a calmer state of mind and that will relieve your vulnerability in a harsh and competitive world, to the extent that it has the complete opposite effect on the human psyche as what it is searching for simply doesn't exist, causing the mind to step into a state of anxiety.

Certainty Doesn't Exist

Let's take a step back in time to an era in history when food was either gathered in nature, hunted down, or grown by yourself. Water sources had to be found, secured, and protected to ensure one's livelihood. One's survival depended on having access to the necessary supplies to keep one alive, and certainty about having access to such sources would surely improve one's odds of survival.

We no longer have to source our basic needs in such a primitive manner, and having certainty about your next paycheck, that there will be light when you flip the switch, that there will be food on the shelves in your local

---

1 Manson, M. (2016). *The subtle art of not giving a f*ck : a counterintuitive approach to living a good life*. Harper One, an imprint of HarperCollins Publishers.

supermarket, and that clean water is running from your taps does make life a heck of a lot easier.

Hence, the motivation to pursue certainty has been passed on to us from our ancestors, as it is what helped them secure their survival. However, as much as our ancestors had no control over whether a flood was going to destroy their crops or if an animal would kill them while out hunting, we, too, have no real certainty today. Retrenchments happen, sickness happens, accidents happen, and these things are all a threat to certainty. But ultimately, it is the lens through which you perceive the world that generates the greatest sense of uncertainty. When you embrace life's inherent uncertainties rather than viewing them through the lens of fear, you are much more likely to experience a pressing desire for certainty.

The Psychological Toll of Hanging on to Control

Dr. Steven Stosny explains that for the brain to establish a state of certainty, it needs to filter out a lot of information, often more than it processes, to come to a reasonable conclusion. That means that a lot of vital information is getting lost. This loss of information increases the risk of error, especially during states when emotionally aroused. Hence, during these moments when we're vulnerable to making mistakes, *the need for certainty increases the risk of making mistakes*, putting us in a state of greater vulnerability.[2]

Another approach to exploring the emotional load the need for certainty brings is that it *increases our cognitive burden*. While you may consider yourself a master in multitasking, the reality remains that humans are simply not wired to manage many tasks at once. In psychological terms, the explanation

---

2   Stosny, S. (2021, September 22). *The epidemic of certainty*. Psychology Today. https://www.psychologytoday.com/za/blog/anger-in-the-age-entitlement/202109/the-epidemic-certainty

for this limitation is that we're not geared to have a wide cognitive range. The search for certainty often consists of desperate attempts and grabbing onto a range of unrelated matters in the desire to find certainty. This frantic search and instant connection lead to what we call an increased cognitive burden, contributing to *an emotional and mental drain*. In this state, your mind is already so overloaded and preoccupied that you're *not prepared to deal with other matters life throws at you*, not even insignificant ones.

Embracing Uncertainty and Finding Peace

The most prominent obstacle keeping us from embracing uncertainty is the fear and anxiety it provokes. Hence, as soon as you can manage these feelings and overcome the weight of anxiety, it becomes easier to embrace uncertainty. It is how you simultaneously overcome the anxiety that your frantic search for certainty has caused.

The breathing techniques explored in Chapter One can help you embrace uncertainty and find inner peace. The mindfulness exercises covered in Chapter Three are another helpful aid to overcome the anxiety associated with the perceived loss of certainty. You can also use journaling to process your thoughts, which will also bring relief. However, there is another specific form of meditation that will help you overcome the secondary or second arrow challenge evoked by the need for certainty.

Overcoming the Second Arrow Challenge with Body Scan Meditation

The concept of *the second arrow* is derived from a Buddhist parable stating that every challenge in life is two-fold. The first arrow is the actual problem, hitting its target. These arrows are bound to hit you in life, and you have little to no control over them. But then there is the second arrow: your response to what has happened and, specifically, how you feel as it robs you of your certainty. These feelings tend to be far more detrimental to your overall well-being. However, it is something you can control. The second arrow parable implies that it isn't the problem you're facing that is the problem but how you respond to the problem.

While the origin of the second arrow is the mind, its negative impact can be felt in the body as it causes stress and anxiety, leading to increased physical discomfort and pain. This is where body scan meditation is a helpful aid to overcome physical negativity.

- Find a quiet spot where you can sit comfortably without disturbance.
- Close your eyes and set your intention on having a helpful meditative session.
- Breathe deeply a few times to relax your body and clear your mind.
- Visualize a scanner and the bright light with which it scans a document.
- With this image in mind, start scanning your body. Begin at the crown of your head, noticing how you're feeling. Without any judgment, simply take note of any signs of stress, stiffness, pain, or discomfort you may feel.
- Then, decide to release the tension within. Allow your muscles to relax and the pain and discomfort to ease out of your body.
- Once you're aware of the state of the specific area, move your scanning mental eye to the next section.
- Progress through your face, neck, shoulders, arms, chest, and torso before going onto your belly, lower back, hips, thighs, knees, calves, and ankles until you're finally at the tips of your toes.

As you release tension and pain from your body, allow anxiety to flow from your mind. Realize that your certainty was merely based on expectations. While expectations are good to have, they're nothing more than a mere wish of how you want things to be. This is how you can use your body to control your emotional response, allowing you to let go of the need for certainty and embrace the many uncertainties in life.

Chapter 14

Trusting the Process

Trust the wait. Embrace the uncertainty. Enjoy the beauty of becoming. When nothing is certain, anything is possible.

—Mandy Hale

The word trust means to have confidence in someone or something outside of yourself. It implies a willingness to surrender the need to have certainty. It is also closely associated with giving up attempts to enforce control, as the desire for control is often futile. Due to the confidence you have, you're more open to accepting risk and staying vulnerable in the situation.

To have trust means that while you believe all will work out well in the end, you're open to any outcome, and therefore, you can freely renounce the need for certainty. As this inspires a willingness to embrace any situation, you're bound to experience more diversity in life, learn unexpected things, and grow personally. The willingness to accept uncertainty in your life makes life more exciting while pushing boundaries and forcing you to step outside your comfort zone.

The Benefits of Surrendering

In the context of warfare, the word surrender is commonly perceived in a negative light as it implies you've been outplayed, outperformed, and outwitted. But in the context of certainty and trusting your inherent wisdom, it is best to step away from this very legit interpretation of the word to explore more meaningful definitions of the term. I am specifically thinking in the context of surrendering to the inherent wisdom of the universe and trusting in divine timing. In this context, surrendering is a powerful choice, enabling you to reap several outstanding benefits. about surrendering to the universe's inherent wisdom.

When surrendering is understood as letting go of negative emotions, expectations, resistance, and attachments, it becomes a powerful step toward ultimate holistic well-being and an improved quality of life.

- *Inner peace.* Once you let go of all resistance and surrender to what is happening in the given moment—what has been planned for you in the universe to happen according to divine timing—a deep and overcoming inner peace sets in.

- *Increased freedom.* The quest for control has a bitter irony in that the more you try to gain it, the more the subject of your obsession gains control over you. The more you seek it, the more the subject of your obsession has control over you. But once you let go of the need to control and opt to surrender, the freedom you experience increases organically.

- *Greater resilience.* Surrendering means allowing yourself the flexibility to roll with the punches life is directing at you. The more you miss the punches, the longer you'll stand upright in the boxing ring of life, showing greater resilience to the challenges you're facing.

- *Healthier relationships.* Surrendering brings about several side benefits, improving your life in the most unexpected ways. Some of these involve greater compassion for others as it becomes easier to step into their shoes. This increased compassion contributes to an increased ability to show forgiveness and contributes to forging stronger bonds.

Letting Go of Attachments

Surrendering means, to a large extent, letting go of unhealthy attachments. In our context, these attachments are mostly emotional attachments, referring to the strong emotional bonds you have with something or someone else. Often, these attachments allow you to enjoy a sense of closeness with or feel a deep sense of affection for someone or something, which is good, but not all types of attachment are positive.

There are four types of attachments to consider.

- *Secure attachments* can be found in relationships you have with those you trust and rely on. These form as your trust in the other person expands, and your confidence in the relationship grows stronger. It is the kind of attachment that fosters a physical and/or emotional dependence on another.
- *Anxious attachments* develop when uncertainty steps in, and you start to doubt the people or things you trust. This uncertainty causes an increased sense of anxiety, meaning the attachment is no longer healthy to sustain.
- *Avoidant attachment* occurs when you deliberately avoid closeness or trust with another to keep yourself from feeling hurt or disappointed.
- *Disorganized attachment* is often associated with a wide range of mixed feelings sparked by a specific bond or connection. The emotional uncertainty it brings contributes to increased stress and anxiety.

Dr. Mike Brooks reminds us that attachment can be a double-edged sword and that you need to hold onto it loosely. He reminds us of an ancient Buddhist truth known as the *Four Noble Truths*. These four truths state that:

- All life is suffering.
- Suffering is the result of attachment, often in the form of desire or craving.
- Suffering ends once you let go of the attachment.
- There is only one path away from craving, desire, and attachment: the *Noble Eightfold Path*.

The *Noble Eightfold Path* is a Buddhist guideline to a life freed from the emotional strain attachment places on you. It can serve as a reminder to practice greater awareness of being mindful, applying awareness of your perspective, intention, the way you talk, your actions, how you choose to live, the level of effort you commit yourself to, and your level of concentration on matters.

Once all of these are aligned with embracing uncertainty, you step into a state of non-attachment, meaning you're letting go of the attachments that keep you in a state of desire for certainty and control over life. It brings about a greater sense of inner peace.

Techniques to Recognize and Release Attachments

Not all attachments are bad, and there are surely some you would want to hold onto and even nurture. However, there are also many attachments that don't serve you at all, and to recognize these and release them demands a deep commitment to self-reflection.

Self-reflection is a mindfulness technique that is best practiced daily. However, the rushed pace of modern life often keeps us from allowing ourselves the time for self-reflection. It may also be that you desire to get to know yourself better through self-reflection but are finding it immensely hard to get going with this practice.

At the end of Part Five, I am sharing 20 questions to encourage deep self-reflection. Use these questions to guide you toward an inner journey. Reflect on your answers by capturing your thoughts in a journal, as then you can revert to them as necessary. It will also provide you with a record of your thoughts and enable you to notice changes and improvements.

Mindfulness Meditation to Let Go of Attachment

Mindfulness meditation is a useful strategy to achieve a range of beneficial outcomes. One of these is breaking free from the attachments holding you back in life.

The following mindfulness meditation will help you to have a lighter awareness of your experiences and circumstances, enabling you to perceive matters from a different perspective.

1. Find a place where you can enjoy undisturbed peace and calmness.
2. Settle down in a comfortable position.
3. Close your eyes while using deep breathing to notice triggers of restlessness. Acknowledge these triggers before nudging them gently from your mind to keep them from distracting you.
4. Tune in to your internal chatter to see if there are any repetitive messages.
5. Look at your inner chatter merely to observe it without judging or engaging with it.
6. Mentally label this chatter as comments without any specific purpose or relevance.
7. Shift your focus to how you're feeling today.

8. Be aware of your feelings without judgment or trying to determine why you're experiencing certain emotions.

9. Label these feelings as mere emotions without attaching any deeper meaning to them.

10. Notice the distance you created between yourself and your thoughts and feelings by labeling them.

11. Shift your focus to switching from seeing thoughts and feelings as problems to being merely aware of their existence.

12. Try to detect a decline in the thoughts and feelings you notice as you distance yourself from them.

13. Enjoy how much easier it becomes to accept matters as they are once you've created some distance between yourself and your thoughts and feelings by labeling them and calling them what they are.

In the words of Brittany Hallison, author of *Letting Go: Surrender, Release Attachments & Accept the Present*, "The solution to all our stresses and anxieties and the key to true happiness is letting go of all our needless attachments. If we let go of our need to be beautiful, we do not let that stubborn facial acne or that dry skin ruin our day. If we let go of the desire for everyone to like us, we do not become frustrated when people do not. If we let go of the need for the house to be spotless, we can focus on what genuinely matters in our lives. We don't have to become careless about our appearance, let our houses become a mess, or be rude to others - but we don't need to let these aspects of our lives cause us suffering either. We just need to be."[1]

Through greater acceptance, it becomes easier to surrender to those things you can't control. It becomes easier to enjoy the life you deserve.

---

1 Hallison, B. L. (2015). *Letting Go*. Createspace Independent Publishing Platform.

Chapter 15
Embracing Surrender

The moment of surrender is not when life is over. It's when it begins.

—Marianne Williamson

The simplest explanation of the word surrender is to stop resisting an enemy and to submit to their authority. However, when I urge you to surrender, I'm not encouraging you to hand over your power to an enemy. No, surrendering in our context is about acknowledging that you're up against a force much stronger than you and keeping in mind that the force you're up against isn't out to get you.

What Are You Up Against?

Recently, my sister and her husband got a new addition to their family: Cheeky. Cheeky is a ball of excitement and energy wrapped up in the softest fluff. She loves to be spoiled and has boundless energy. It is often the latter that gets her into trouble, as she will (and has done so several times already) chew on anything she finds if there is no outlet for her energy.

I was visiting them for a Sunday barbeque, and while there were several people around to play with Cheeky, we were all mostly involved in adult conversation, and Cheeky had to settle for pats here and there. At some point during the barbeque, I realized that Cheeky was no longer jumping up against legs, begging for attention. It was then that my eye wandered across the garden to see if I could spot the little ball of mischief, and I did. Fortunately, she wasn't busy getting herself into trouble but was on an entirely different quest.

Cheeky had found a way to keep herself busy. A few weeks prior, a strong wind blew over a medium-sized tree on the furthest end of the yard. It uprooted the tree, causing some of the roots to be revealed above the soil surface. Here, Cheeky had found herself a root and was desperately trying to pull it closer to her bed, entirely unaware of the fact that at the other end of the root, a whole tree was attached. Yet, that didn't stop her from exerting all her energy on this impossible quest. She continued to pull and tug on this root, to no avail, until there was no energy left in her tiny body, and she simply tipped amidst her quest to take a nap.

Watching from a distance, it was easy to see Cheeky was busy with an impossible quest. However, during the moments when we behave in exactly the same way, it is much harder to see our mistake and that we're really fighting a force much larger than ourselves. Not all, but often, the battles we exert our mental, emotional, and physical energy on simply can't be won, and while we may try for as long as we want, we're only wasting our energy.

In *The Surrender Experiment: My Life Journey into Life's Perfection*, author Michael A. Singer reminds us, "Life rarely unfolds exactly as we want it to. And if we stop and think about it, that makes perfect sense. The scope of life is universal, and the fact that we are not actually in control of life's events should be self-evident. The universe has been around for 13.8 billion years, and the processes that determine the flow of life around us did not begin when we were born, nor will they end when we die."[1]

---

1 Singer, M. A. (2015). *The surrender experiment : my journey into life's perfection*. Harmony Books.

Why do I urge you to surrender? The alternative is a futile effort that will rob you of internal peace, a peace that can only be found once you let go of all resistance and allow the universe, life, events, and unforeseen circumstances to take you to new, unexpected, and exhilarating places.

The Power of Surrendering

Surrendering is always accompanied by *releasing resistance* and *finding inner peace*. But there is more to surrendering and letting go of the unnecessary attachments you burden yourself with. Yet too many refuse to surrender because they see it as a sign of weakness, a curse word, equating it to giving up. I am not in denial about how hard it can be to surrender. In *A Return to Love*, author Marianne Williamson explains how surrendering often only takes place when we reach our lowest point in life. She states that it is only once our knees are knocked from beneath us that we stop playing at life and truly start living.[2] She states that once this happens, fear might step in, as for the first time in probably forever, you realize the importance of living, that you only live once and that there is no more time for playing around. Surrendering often happens when you think your life is over, but it is truly the beginning of living fully. So, when it seems that your life is falling apart, stand back, for in reality, it may just be falling into place for the first time ever.

- *Shifting your focus.* Surrendering will empower you to stop fixating on the things you can't change, freeing up your mind and time so that you can actively start working on the things you can change. It is only once you direct your energy in such a productive manner that you can truly make a difference in life—yours and that of those around you. By letting go, you're truly claiming your power.
- *Living in the present.* Surrendering means that whatever happened in the past or what you expect (perhaps even fear) to happen in the future no longer matters, as you've relinquished any perceived control you may have over matters. It means no other time becomes as important as the present,

---

2   Williamson, M. (2016). *A Return to Love*. HarperOne.

and once you start living in the present, you will reap many more benefits. Like seeing things as they truly are and having less stress in your life.

- *Reclaiming your power.* What will happen when you're set free from the shackles holding you back in life? Once you finally surrender and let go of what Brené Brown refers to as counterfeit control, you'll be able to identify the things you have control over and apply all your resources to make the most of those things. It is then that you reclaim your power and step into the fullness of your being, living according to your purpose.

Surrendering, letting go, may initially sound like a passive process, like giving up. However, we've learned that it is very much an active process, a decision that will leave you more empowered than ever before. The truly successful people in life have conquered their fears of surrendering.

"God, grant me the serenity to accept the things I cannot change, courage to change the things I can, and wisdom to know the difference." These words of wisdom from the *Serenity Prayer* have been helping alcoholics and addicts turn around their lives for decades. The prayer, urging us to surrender to those things we have no control over and enabling us to take control of those things that are within our power to change, has been the cornerstone of addiction recovery. Surrendering equates to stepping into your power. That is the paradoxical nature of surrendering.

Five Steps to Surrendering

No two people are exactly alike, and therefore, there is no limited number of techniques you must follow to surrender yourself and step into your power. You do what you need to do, but I would like to share the following mindfulness tips, as they are helpful to remember on your journey to finding your best way to ultimate freedom.

What Scares You?

It often helps to ask, "What is the worst that can happen?" When you do, it will most likely become evident that the worst isn't as bad as you initially perceived it to be. Identifying the worst possible outcome will also enable you to prepare yourself for what may happen in advance. Such preparation may not necessarily be something practical, as at times, we also have to prepare ourselves emotionally to deal with loss or transformation.

Be Patient

Be patient with yourself and allow sufficient time for the process to unfold naturally. Surrendering and letting go of the things you can't change so that you can step into your power is a massive shift in life and may pivot you in an entirely different (even opposite at times) direction than what you've been used to until this point in your life.

It takes about a week for a butterfly egg to hatch and the caterpillar to appear. After another 12–14 days, the larva turns into a pupa, and it is only after 7–10 more days that the butterfly emerges from the cocoon. So, we're looking at about 4–5 weeks of change, growth, and transformation for the butterfly to achieve its full potential and beauty and to live according to the purpose it has in the world. Typically, an adult butterfly lives for only 2–6 weeks, meaning it takes almost as long to become the butterfly it was supposed to be as it has to be what it was intended to become.

There are two things that stand out for me about the lifecycle of the butterfly. The first is that transformation takes time, often quite a lot of time, in relation to the rest of life. The second point is that regardless of how long it takes to become what you're supposed to be, it is always worth the time and effort, so be patient with yourself. There is no rush in the process.

Identify the Things You Have Control Over

Just as essential as recognizing the things you can't control and acknowledging that you have no power over these matters is identifying the things you can control. What are the things that you have an influence over? What matters can you control, but are you experiencing limited control as someone else meddles in your business? How can you reclaim control in these areas?

Dream About Freedom

What does ultimate freedom look like to you? We all have different ideas about what a perfect life would look like. Similarly, there are different things that excite us, make us happy, and also upset us. These differences exist and are linked to the uniqueness of all. As these differences exist, it is important to acknowledge that my idea of ultimate freedom may not even resemble what your perception of freedom looks like. Therefore, you need to identify what freedom means to you.

- Visualize what a free future looks like to you.
- Dream about it in as much detail as possible.
- Jot down your expectations for living in such a state of freedom.
- List the things that are keeping you from stepping into such a state of freedom.

While these steps will give you greater clarity and direction in your quest to enjoy greater freedom, they will also help you identify the obstacles in your way and the matters you have to let go of to enjoy this freedom.

Finding Freedom in Acceptance

Acceptance removes the sting of the second arrow. It enables us to *accept life for what it is* and teaches us how to *make the best* of it by *navigating us through the challenges life* brings with peace, strength, and the resilience to keep going, even when it is hard. Through acceptance, you can *embrace pain and learn from it.*

I was about 9 or 10 when it hit me. Initially, it was only mild discomfort I woke up with one morning. I can't even recall telling my mom about it. However, as the days and later weeks went by, it became more intense. Initially, my mother rubbed my legs with all kinds of ointments and applied hot packs to relieve my pain. Later on, we tried cold packs, too, but these aids only brought some relief. One night, it was so bad that I went to bed crying. I am not sure if that was the reason for the first visit to the doctor, but I do remember that he finally had the answer we were looking for: growth pains. That was the answer.

I remember looking at the man, who seemed to be almost the same age as my granddad, who had passed away the previous year, when he said over the brim of his glasses, "You're just growing very fast right now."

How was that supposed to help me? "How do I grow slower?" I asked.

"You can't stop the natural processes of nature, but I can promise you that even in nature, the most amazing and beautiful creatures also have to experience pain to become what they are. Try to think about your pain as an investment in becoming the best version of yourself. You'll become tall, fast, great at sports, and perhaps a model. Those are all things you may become," he tried to pacify me.

I didn't get so tall after all. Nor did I become fast, excellent in sports, and heck, I am not even close to being a model, but I did learn one valuable lesson from this excursion, which took the better half of a year: growing hurts, regardless of whether you're 9 going on 10, or at any other stage in life.

Growth hurts, but once you embrace it as part of your journey, it becomes a highly useful teacher. Facing your pain, whether physical, emotional, or mental, helps you understand yourself a bit better. It guides you to your unique spot in the world and shows you how to make the most of what life has to offer despite the hardships you face. Once you've gained these insights, it is impossible not to excel in life. The freedom such acceptance brings is unparalleled.

Radical Acceptance vs Resignation

Do not confuse radical acceptance with resignation. The two terms are nothing but opposites of each other. While radical acceptance brings freedom, positivity, and peace, resignation is riddled with negative emotions.

Radical acceptance says, "I acknowledge the things I can't change and accept them so that I no longer have to sacrifice inner peace or waste time and energy on matters beyond my control. I can preserve my limited resources to focus on matters I have control over, and that leaves me with inner peace and a sense of empowerment.

In contrast, resignation states, "I am giving up and am no longer trying to change the situation in my favor, not because I choose to do so to enable myself to prosper, but because I feel forced to do so." Resignation tends to leave the person resigning with feelings of frustration, sadness, anger, injustice, and fear.

Radical acceptance is a way to free yourself, while resignation means losing faith in the belief that life can be better. It is what gives us permission to authentically express who we are.

Cultivating Acceptance Through Mindfulness

Throughout the book, we've explored various mindfulness exercises and forms of meditation that are all helpful aids to focusing your thoughts in the present moment. In these moments of clarity and stillness, you can embrace acceptance of yourself, others, and the world.

The first step to claiming your superpower is to make the deliberate choice to actively pursue acceptance. It is important to identify your personal reasons for wanting to pursue radical acceptance because, as I mentioned, growth is painful.

Identify your resistance against acceptance. The better you are at identifying the obstacles keeping you from achieving your goal, the easier it is to overcome or bypass them. Often, the ego is at the heart of resistance as it desires complete control, and acceptance demands surrendering control. The only way to bypass the ego is to allow your awareness to be nestled within your soul, seeking freedom instead of the ego's desire to maintain counterfeit control over the world.

Become actively involved in acceptance. In contrast to resignation, acceptance demands activity. It requires identifying what matters are best accepted and which matters deserve fighting for and then doing just that: fighting for what is important.

Increase awareness of opportunities for acceptance. Mindfulness and meditation will increase your awareness of opportunities, allowing you to practice radical acceptance regularly and turn it into a habit.

20 Questions/Prompts Leading You to Deep Self-Reflection

Complete the following exercise in your journal. You should also consider getting a self-reflection journal where you focus only on getting familiar with every aspect of your being.

It is best to write down the question and your answers, as that will make it easier to revert to your questions and to notice how your answers change through personal development.

Lists

1. List 30 things that make you happy. These don't have to be expensive or huge. Simple things like the smell of a cup of coffee can make you smile, too.
2. List five people you rely on and trust to always be there for you.
3. List three memories that have taught you valuable lessons in life.
4. List 10 words that best describe who you are.

Questions

1. What are my five greatest strengths?
2. What does unconditional love look like?
3. What qualities in others do I admire?
4. What are five things I can't live without?
5. How am I different in public compared to being at home?
6. What do I hope for in life?
7. How do I want people to see me?
8. What animal best represents my personality? Why?

Prompts

1. I feel stressed when...
2. I wish I was more...
3. I do my best when...
4. I am being hard on myself when...
5. I can be myself with...
6. Life should be all about...
7. I wish I could...
8. I am courageous when...

Part 6

Untangling Your Emotions

Sometimes emotions are layered like an onion, and while you have to work on one to get to the next, there is some order. But as easily, the inner landscape of emotions can resemble a bowl of spaghetti and it is much harder to determine where one feeling ends and the next begins.

It is time to explore how to process emotions in healthy ways, especially during challenging times in life. We're also digging into the significance of connecting to one's emotions and recognizing the intelligence stored within both the mind and body.

Chapter 16

Recognizing the Complexity of Emotions

Human beings have so many complex emotions. If you just leave them to run riot, most people will become insane.

—Sadhguru

In 2015, the world met Riley. Riley was a young girl whose life got turned upside down when her parents packed up their lives in a Midwest town and moved to San Francisco. It was a major adjustment for the young girl, who was already facing the hardships of growing up without the skill of being emotionally mature. The sudden and drastic changes in her home environment caused her emotions to run rampant.

Of course, I am referring to the plot of the animated film Inside Out. If you haven't seen it yet, please do so before watching the sequel, which will be released in 2024 (at the time of writing).

Riley's life revolves around five main emotions: anger, sadness, disgust, fear, and joy, but in reality, we have a much wider range of emotions to manage. Still, the animation offers a deeper perspective on how various emotions can impact each other and how we may, at times, believe what we're feeling is one thing when, in reality, it is another.

The complexity of emotions is both daunting and exhausting. It can lead to poor decisions, inappropriate behavior, and saying things we later regret. Unless you have a clear understanding of what every emotion entails, can acknowledge what you're feeling and why, and know how to manage it effectively, feelings can take control of your life and leave you in a dire situation.

The Intricate Nature of Human Emotions

Dr. Steven Stosny, author of multiple books on relationships and the founder of Compassion Power, sheds some light on the complex nature of emotions. "Emotions emerged over a much longer evolutionary history than language. Along the way, they developed considerable complexity that can easily confound social interactions." He then further expands on some of the elements that contributed to the complex nature of emotions, namely habitation, inhibition, constriction, and disinhibition or excitement.[1]

1. *Habitation.* The more you do something, the more it becomes a habit, enabling you to do something or respond in a certain manner almost automatically. Dr. Stosny explains that by the time most of us reach adulthood, we have developed certain set responses to a wide range of triggers, meaning we no longer think about our feelings but have an emotional response on cue, causing us to express our feelings as we've practiced over several years.

---

1   Stosny, S. (2017, April 8). *Emotional complexity* . Psychology Today. https://www.psychologytoday.com/us/blog/anger-in-the-age-entitlement/201704/emotional-complexity#:~:text=Emotions%20emerged%20over%20a%20much

2. *Inhibition*. Some feelings prevent us from expressing other feelings. For instance, the empathy you have toward your partner for just being fired may keep you from expressing your excitement over your recent promotion. Certain feelings act as stronger inhibitors than others, and at the top of the list are fear and shame as the most powerful inhibiting emotions.

3. *Constriction*. One feeling can work against another, causing the two feelings to cancel each other out while causing an immense level of internal friction. Let's say that despite your desire to travel because you've always wanted to see the world, your nagging guilt over leaving a sick parent's bedside behind is preventing you from taking the trip.

4. *Disinhibition*. Some feelings make others stronger. Dr. Stosny explains that we can only experience excitement when fear or shame is present to a lesser extent. While this may sound completely illogical, the following explanation will demonstrate the complex nature of feelings. Excitement is the result of being exposed to experiencing the unpleasant emotions of fear or shame but then escaping the situation without being exposed to either. For instance, the excitement of winning another sports team is linked to the shame of losing to them. The excitement of jumping out of a plane at several thousand feet is linked to the fear of dying. Without fear or shame, excitement simply won't exist.

Why We Suppress Feelings (And the Harm it Brings)

Habitation, inhibition, construction, and inhibition aren't the only contributing factors to the complex nature of our feelings. Another factor to consider is the suppression of feelings. It is important to understand how suppressing your feelings impacts your responses and how it has a far-reaching negative impact on you.

Some feelings, positive and negative, are fleeting, and it is easy to suppress them, but others have a way of lingering for much longer. These longer-lasting negative feelings can make life unpleasant and, at times, may force us to acknowledge and confront certain aspects of ourselves or our lives that we would rather avoid. The best way to stay in denial is to simply suppress these feelings. Hence, we can safely say that emotional suppression is a psychological defense mechanism we use to block out emotional pain. However, while it may appear to be the safer option, suppressed feelings tend to cause far more severe and lasting harm. A much safer solution is acknowledging and confronting unpleasant feelings and processing them out of your mind and life.

To fully grasp the negative impact of emotional suppression, we have to dig in and explore what happens under the surface when blocking out negative emotions. Emotions may have a physical response in the body, but ultimately, they originate in the mind. Once these thoughts surface in the mind and you're committed to blocking them out, the most natural response is to speak to yourself rather abruptly and with immense blame and harshness to stop thinking in a certain manner.

It is usually only once you apply mindfulness and increased awareness of your internal chatter that you'll notice the rude and critical way you may address yourself to keep these feelings from lingering. Some statements that come to mind are, "Stop it! What is wrong with me?" or "You're such a fool for feeling this way."

It's not so nice now, is it?

The result?

Even more negative emotions begin to surface. While your approach did nothing to resolve the original negative feelings, as you didn't process them at all, you've now also generated even more critical and harmful feelings, mostly linked to self-criticism, causing a decline in confidence and self-esteem.

By refraining from practicing effective emotional management skills, you're also slowing down the growth and development of your emotional intelligence.

Defining Emotional Intelligence

Over recent years, the term emotional intelligence, or emotional quotient (EQ), has gained more traction due to a growing awareness of its role in success in your personal and professional lives. Often, in mainstream media articles, EQ is compared with its predecessor and the previous determining factor of success, IQ, or intelligence quotient.

When we explore the true meaning of emotional intelligence beyond perceiving it as merely a buzzword, we learn that EQ refers to the ability to effectively and constructively understand, interpret, and respond to feelings while also being able to communicate them clearly.

Do you have a naturally high EQ? The following are all indicators of high emotional intelligence:

- Confidence and self-acceptance.
- A strong sense of curiosity.
- Sensitivity toward the feelings of others.
- Emotional awareness and the ability to quickly and accurately identify what others are feeling.
- Taking responsibility for your mistakes.
- Effective emotional management, especially in challenging situations.

Not so much describing you? Not to worry, as while some people have inherently higher emotional intelligence, it is very much a learned skill, and you can work on your ability to manage your feelings.

In *The Body Keeps The Score*, Dr. Bessel van der Kolk explores the physical impact negative emotions, specifically trauma, have on the body.[2] He explains in the book, "While we all want to move beyond trauma, the part of our brain that is devoted to ensuring our survival (deep below our rational brain) is not very good at denial. Long after a traumatic experience is over, it may be reactivated at the slightest hint of danger, mobilize disturbed brain circuits, and secrete massive amounts of stress hormones. This precipitates unpleasant emotions, intense physical sensations, and impulsive and aggressive actions... Feeling out of control, survivors of trauma often begin to fear that they are damaged to the core and beyond redemption."

The emotional response Dr. Van der Kolk is talking about is present in the limbic system. The limbic system, consisting of the amygdala, hippocampus, and parts of the midbrain, is present from birth onwards and is biologically tasked with the responsibility of storing every emotion and impression even long before we're capable of expressing our feelings or thinking about the deeper meaning behind them. This specific brain area is the emotional warehouse in the body, and from here, every memory gains meaning.

The rational or logical thinking brain develops and matures later, forming around the limbic system. So, every rational thought is always impacted by the emotions in the limbic system. It is how the biological structure of the brain supports the mind-body connection.

Through the mind-body connection, the mind impacts the body by means of hormonal secretion, creating various physical responses. However, this communication channel allows for two-way communication, as the body can also impact the mind through this connection, meaning you can

---

2   Van Der Kolk, B. (2015). *The body keeps the score: Brain, mind, and body in the healing of trauma*. Penguin Books.

use your body to establish and maintain a greater sense of emotional calm. So, you can use your body as an effective tool for emotional management.

Connecting With Your Emotional Landscape

Before you can connect with your emotional landscape, you need to identify and gain clarity on what it is you're connecting to. This brings us to the question: What is the emotional landscape? A simple definition of the term would be that it is the map of emotions you often feel. These are emotions you're used to, familiar with, and comfortable with, and hence would often fall back on when the need for emotional expression arises.

For instance, the young man brought up with the now fortunately archaic and hopefully soon-to-be extinct motto of 'boys don't cry' may revert to anger whenever he is emotionally aroused, as anger was the only emotion deemed acceptable during his formative years. So, when someone cuts him off in traffic, he responds with anger. When his dog dies, he responds with anger. When he gets a devastating diagnosis, he responds with anger.

Essentially, due to his upbringing, the young man is living within a very limited and restricting emotional landscape. Since he has never been allowed, given permission, or encouraged to spread his wings and explore other emotions, he remains emotionally crippled.

Why You Need to Make the Connection

Returning to school from summer break, one of my great friends, Sarah, was smitten. Her summer love was so remarkable that anyone with ears had to hear about it every moment we spent together. We were 16, and while we thought we were as clever as could be, we really knew nothing. Either way, the one phrase she kept on saying about her latest love was that he was so *emotionally connected*.

Honestly, I started to feel physically sick every time I heard it. Firstly, because I think I heard it 200 times; secondly, because of my young ignorance, I didn't fully comprehend the importance of being connected to your emotions; and thirdly, I didn't think Sarah understood it either, and I felt her new love turned my good friend into a clumsy, pretentious mess.

I was wrong. So was Sarah. Connecting with your emotions is a wonderful attribute essential to personal development and living your best life.

- *Knowing your why*. Emotions are your internal compass, directing you toward what you feel, why you feel a certain way, and how to best navigate the journey you're on. It provides guidance and clarity during decision-making and helps us figure out life and what we want from it.

- It brings a *sense of control*. Emotional connection and familiarity with your guidance system help you better manage your life and leave you with a sense of control. It also increases your confidence in your ability to navigate life successfully.

- It *prevents negative thoughts from running rampant*. Negative feelings and negative thoughts are two peas in a pod. Where one is, so is the other. You may find it hard to control your thoughts, but if you can control your feelings by acknowledging their presence early on, identifying why you feel a certain way, and learning how to resolve these feelings, you can also clamp down on negative thoughts.

- It *helps you to understand your needs*. Knowing what you feel and why you feel that way makes it easier to identify what you need to resolve these feelings. With this understanding, it becomes far easier to know what you need to get better, and you'll also have the confidence to ask for what you need.

- *You connect better with others.* The better you understand your emotions, the easier it becomes to correctly identify feelings in others. This enables you to support them effectively and, therefore, strengthen your bonds.

Tuning In to Your Emotions

Due to these many benefits, effectively tuning in to your feelings is a must to support effective emotional management.

Returning to the movie Inside Out, we can learn a lot, even as adults, from how emotions and the physical impact have been portrayed. Once you start to notice each feeling as an entity in its own right, it becomes easier to attach various features to it, which will help you to understand the feeling, what triggered it, and how to best manage it.

The next couple of practices are all directed to help you gain a similar understanding of your wide range of emotions, as depicted in the movie.

- *Turn your feelings into an image.* Grab a piece of paper, crayons, coloring pencils, or even paint, and create an image representing your current emotional state. Are you angry like an exploding volcano? Perhaps you're enjoying a state of calm, and the image that comes to mind is one of willow trees edging a lake. What does your emotional landscape look like at the moment? Give it some thought, and then have fun recreating your mental image on paper.
- *Address your emotions.* If you perceive your emotions as independent entities, it becomes easier to address them directly. Find a quiet spot to turn within so that you can connect with your feelings. Ask your feelings why they're present, what caused them to surface, and what they want you to do. While feelings will never give you an answer, pondering on your emotions in this childlike manner will increase

your familiarity with what you're feeling, reduce the anxiety negative feelings may provoke, and enable you to address and manage these feelings effectively.

Using Your Mind-Body Connection to Your Benefit

Earlier, I touched on the mind-body connection, but as this connection is such a helpful aid to connect with and improve your emotional state by using your body, we have to allow for greater exploration and guidance on how to make it work for you.

Every emotion we feel manifests as a physical sensation inside the body. Some are more prevalent, like feeling butterflies in your stomach when you're nervous or burning up when you're angry. Sadness is associated with a drop in body temperature, while happiness is associated with a comfortable warmth.

Lauri Nummenmaa, a molecular neuroscientist, explains that this happens because emotions are more than a mere mental state; they manifest as bodily states, too. The mind-body connection exists to prepare the body to respond to any threats swiftly and is, in this way, an aid to survival. While the mind-body connection was immensely helpful to our ancestors facing many life-threatening situations, we, as a modern generation, can tap into the connection too and benefit from what it has to offer. Nummenmaa states, "Awareness of the corresponding bodily changes may subsequently trigger the conscious emotional sensations, such as the feeling of happiness." It means you can use your body to bring about change in your mind and improve your emotional state, either to bring instant relief by resolving unpleasant emotions, like breathing deeply to reduce anxiety during a panic attack, or it can improve more significant and lasting mental health concerns, as in the case of the following research study.

In a 2011 study, the effectiveness of this connection was proven to be a valuable aid in addressing various emotional challenges. Researchers detected a significant improvement in the depression symptoms of Palestinian children and teens after just 10 sessions in a mind-body skills work group.[3]

These and similar work groups consist of meditation, breathing techniques, biofeedback, guided imagery, and creative expression using self-expression drawings. After just seven months, most of the study participants were freed of the sense of hopelessness that plagued them and better equipped to deal with hardships and challenges.

Biofeedback is an effective tool using electrodes to measure and track the body's physical response to emotions. It also leans toward being a tool to use the body to manipulate feelings, and over recent years, it has turned into an effective tool to manage various mental and emotional challenges and even address mental health concerns. A con of biofeedback is that you'll need to call on the assistance of a professional for this kind of treatment, which may be pricey.

But there are several other mindfulness techniques and strategies you can use at home to deliver similar results. Immediately, I am thinking about meditations, mindfulness exercises, and, specifically, the breathing techniques we explored in Chapter One.

Other solutions can be found in the ancient practices of yoga, tai chi, and qigong. The steady flow of movement increases mental focus and strengthens the bond between mind and body. Through regular practice of any of these, you'll also increase your balance, improve flexibility, and improve your overall

---

3   Selva, J. (2017, January 31). *Exploring the body mind connection (Incl. 5 Techniques)*. Positive Psychology. https://positivepsychology.com/body-mind-integration-attention-training/#:~:text=Practices%20such%20as%20progressive%20muscle

health. Except for qigong, which consists of fewer strenuous stretches and movements, you'll also gain some fitness benefits. A great way to start is by joining a class to learn the correct movement and posture from a trained professional. Once you're more comfortable with the various techniques, you can start practicing them at home, too.

Chapter 17

Embracing Vulnerability and Authenticity

Being vulnerable is the only way to allow your heart to feel true pleasure.

—Bob Marley

Can you recall the last conversation you had when it simply didn't feel like you were connecting to the other person? Perhaps you couldn't pinpoint exactly what it is, but you didn't feel at ease. Sitting through such conversations can be an absolute pain and the discomfort it causes is usually due to the absence of authenticity in the conversation.

The most predominant reason why people refrain from being authentic is because they're scared to be vulnerable. They feel they'll be judged for who they are when they show their true selves. They try to foster new bonds and build their relationships on this fake foundation, and while it may initially appear as if it is working, eventually, it all comes tumbling down.

Four Celebrated Features of Authenticity

Without vulnerability, there is no authenticity, and your personal connections and bonds will suffer.

- *Authenticity inspires empathy.* By being open and honest about your flaws, failures, and fears, you allow others into your world and allow them to step into your shoes, fostering their empathy toward you.

- *Authenticity supports growth.* Only once we acknowledge our shortcomings, faults, and weaknesses can we begin to work on them, supporting personal development.

- *Authenticity increases resilience.* You can lower your stress levels by being more authentic. Life also becomes more enjoyable as your self-esteem gradually increases. A recent study that appeared in Frontiers in Neurology supports these findings, establishing authenticity as a key contributing factor to greater resilience.[1]

- *Authenticity fosters strong connections.* When you allow yourself to open up and be vulnerable by revealing your true self, your weaknesses and shortcomings draw others closer, as your behavior gives them the confidence and certainty that they can reveal their true selves without judgment.

- *Authenticity enables you to cross barriers.* Assumptions and pretense are probably the two most significant barriers blocking the formation of strong and meaningful connections with others. By being authentic and showing your true, flawed self to others, you increase your credibility, and people are more inclined to reach over the barrier and connect with you.

---

1   *How the Merriam-Webster dictionary word of the year helps people build mental resilience.* (2023, November 29). Deseret News. https://www.deseret.com/2023/11/29/23979642/benefits-of-being-authentic/#:~:text=What%20is%20the%20value%20of

Why We Fear Authenticity

Are you a people-pleaser? Do you persistently question your conversations and second-guess your statements? Are you trapped in a persistent state of guilt? Do you often compare yourself to others, only to find yourself falling short?

These are all signs of a lack of authenticity in your interactions with others. It's not easy to be trapped in this web of self-doubt and uncertainty. So, why do it? Because people often find it so much harder to be true to themselves, choosing to live this way seems to be the easy way out.

Why do you avoid being authentic? Are you scared of what you may feel if you are? Are you scared of being ostracized if others see who you really are? Does the idea leave you agonizing over possibly being rejected?

- *We all feel the same (most of us anyway).* The first truth you need to understand is that the majority of people around you harbor the same fears as you do. Take a look at the people around you and know that, in their unique ways, they're as scared as you are about showing who they really are. They may be better at hiding it, but their fears are as real as yours.
- *We're programmed to be fake.* The second point to keep in mind is that, by default, we're programmed to be inauthentic. From a young age, we're taught that society isn't safe and it is best not to reveal your vulnerabilities, as that puts you at risk of being judged, scorned, and criticized. When we observe how this happens to others, sometimes famous people whose lives are dissected for profit in the tabloids, this fear only expands, making it much harder to step into our truth.
- *We try our best to avoid certain feelings.* The third prominent reason that keeps people from being authentic is that we fear feeling all the feelings that go along with being truthful to ourselves. By being inauthentic,

we sedate our emotions and can more effectively suppress those things we don't want to feel. Author Glennon Doyle advises against this safety mechanism when she says, "Being human is not about feeling happy; it's about feeling everything."[2]

Only by experiencing the fullness of emotions can we truly enjoy the richness of humanity and support our personal development.

Embracing Your Vulnerability

How do you overcome years of conditioning to shy away from the truth? Is it even possible? Are you trapped in a state of mental oppression, incapable of ever setting yourself free?

No! Once you identify your lack of authenticity, you can effectively start to address it and step into acceptance, a state where you'll be able to enjoy all the benefits it brings.

Revert to the mindfulness exercises explored in Chapter One to encourage a greater sense of awareness. Once you enter this state and it gradually turns into your common state of being, it is easier to observe the physical manifestation of feelings. Be particularly aware of rising discomfort during interactions to alert you to inauthenticity on your side.

Steps to Overcome the Fear of Authenticity

Only once you acknowledge your lack of authenticity can you start addressing it. The following steps will guide you along the way:

1. Observe yourself intently and notice how your interactions make you feel. If they lead to a sense of growing discomfort, you can now be sure that your adaptive self is speaking. You'll always enjoy a greater sense of ease and comfort when you're authentic.

---

2   Doyle, G. (2020). *Untamed*. The Dial Press.

2. Compare the actions and words of your adaptive self with those of your authentic self, and determine what triggers are causing you to veer off the path of truthfulness.

3. Explore what inspired your inauthentic behavior. For instance, when you catch yourself saying or doing something that leaves you with a sense of discomfort, determine why you're saying it and what the primary cause of fear is keeping you from staying true to yourself. Question, confront, and resolve the cause of fear to set yourself free from it.

You may have to explore even more in-depth practices to overcome the hurdle of fear keeping you from sharing your authentic self with the world, but these three steps will set the course and get you going. Remember to give yourself time. The notion that authenticity needs to be feared has developed over many years, and you won't be able to dismiss it overnight. Rather than rushing the process, enjoy it. Celebrate your progress and be kind to yourself when it is happening slower than you've hoped for.

The Role of Self-Compassion in Dealing With Hard Emotions

Letting go of your adaptive self is a hard but necessary step toward full authenticity. I've mentioned the importance of being kind to yourself when you feel frustrated about your transformation taking place at a slower rate than you envisioned. In Chapter Eight, we explored self-kindness, which falls under the umbrella term of self-compassion, along with humanity and mindfulness.

Now, I want us to pause to see how you can use self-compassion to navigate difficult emotions, making it easier to be authentic but also to reduce the agony confronting such hard emotions often brings.

The Paul Ekman Group advises taking a STANCE when working with difficult emotions. STANCE is the acronym for Stay Tender And Nurture Compassionate Experience.[3]

How do you take a STANCE when facing difficult emotions?

1. *Self-kindness.* Start by treating yourself as if you're your own best friend. We tend to find it much easier to be compassionate toward others than to ourselves, and yet, we deserve to receive as much of our own compassion as others do. When pondering challenging emotions, think about what you would say to yourself if you were your best friend. Consider the tone you use and visualize how your words will make the other person feel. Once you have made the mental shift to be more self-compassionate, it is time to acknowledge what you're experiencing. Admit that you are struggling to deal with your current situation and acknowledge that you don't know how to make it better.

2. *Humanity.* Facing hardship often tumbles us into a state of loneliness. To overcome this sense of isolation, you need to fall back on the humanity leg of self-compassion, meaning you need to acknowledge that hardship and suffering are a part of life and that we are all facing some form of challenge.

3. *Mindfulness.* Lastly, we move onto the mindfulness side of self-compassion, recognizing that while you may experience all these feelings, they don't define your existence or characterize your identity. See these feelings for what they truly are—something you're going through, not who you are.

---

3   Turner, E. (n.d.). *Self-compassion and working with difficult emotions.* Paul Ekman Group. https://www.paulekman.com/blog/self-compassion-working-with-difficult-emotions/#:~:text=Through%20the%20regular%20practice%20of

Common Critical Thoughts Keeping Self-Compassion at Bay

What beliefs and thoughts keep you convinced you're not entitled to self-compassion and kindness?

- *You don't deserve it.* We live in a highly competitive society where there is far more distance than connection than ever before. In many ways, modern society presents a hostile society where it is easy to believe that you don't deserve kindness or that being compassionate is a sign of weakness.

- *You're damaged.* Perhaps you're scared that others will perceive you as damaged or broken when you acknowledge how hard it is for you to deal with your emotions.

- *You're lazy.* While some people fear that others will perceive them as lazy when they choose to be compassionate to themselves, others fear that they will become lazy once they take a break to tend to their emotional needs.

- *You're self-indulgent or self-absorbed.* By choosing yourself and your mental wellness, you can easily be perceived as someone who cares far more about your needs than the greater good of your group.

- *You lack discipline.* Self-kindness can easily be perceived as laziness and lack of the necessary discipline to do what is necessary, making this fear as valid as all the others on this list.

However, these beliefs are all toxic to your mental state and hold the potential to have a detrimental impact on your emotional wellness.

Cultivating Self-Compassion Through Mindfulness

Kristen Neff, co-founder of the Center for Mindfulness Compassion, shares the following steps to a self-compassion break to help you deal effectively with difficult emotions.[4]

1. Find a quiet spot where you can turn within without disturbance.
2. Bring the moment of suffering to mind and acknowledge the pain and stress it brings.
3. Instead of pushing away your pain, embrace it and claim it as yours.
4. Remind yourself that you're not alone in feeling pain and that it is part of life.
5. Place your hands on your heart and notice the warmth of your touch and how soothing it is to your skin.
6. Relax in the moment of comfort while taking a couple of deep breaths.
7. When you're ready and relaxed, you can move on to asking what you need to hear to express kindness to yourself.
8. Identify several statements that may work and notice which is making you feel better. Possible options are:
    a. May I enjoy the kindness I need?
    b. May I allow myself to feel this way?
    c. May I be strong enough to overcome my obstacles?
    d. May I have confidence in myself and my strengths?
9. Keep at this for as long as needed, but before turning to reality, notice the transformation that has been taking place during your self-compassion break and how much stronger you feel to face your challenges.
10. Return to this exercise as often as necessary.

---

4 Neff, K. (n.d.-a). *Exercise 2: Self-Compassion Break*. Self-Compassion. https://self-compassion.org/exercises/exercise-2-self-compassion-break/#:~:text=May%20I%20be%20kind%20to

Chapter 18

Finding Meaning and Growth in Emotional Challenges

Between stimulus and response, there is a space. In that space lies our freedom and power to choose our response. In our response lies our growth and freedom.

—Viktor Frankl

One of my best friends turned 50 recently, and an entire group of ladies headed off to her ranch to enjoy a weekend of celebrations. Many of the ladies decided to travel together, but I still had a late appointment scheduled in the city and had to drive on my own. I didn't mind, as I've been to the ranch many times before and knew the dirt road heading toward the homestead quite well.

The trouble started when I got a frantic call from my friend, saying that the bakery was running late with her cake, and she couldn't wait any longer as she still had some final preparations to make before her guests arrived. She asked if I could stop by the bakery and fetch the triple-layered chocolate mousse cake and bring it along. "Sure!" I said. "Anything for my best friend."

My meeting ran late, and I had to rush through traffic to get in time to the bakery before they closed. I made it in time, but the moment I saw the cake, I knew I had booked myself some trouble. It was a tall tower of cake, and the mousse keeping the layers intact didn't look sturdy enough to stop the cake from toppling over.

However, I persevered and could finally hit a couple of miles out to the ranch by sunset. It meant that when I got to the dirt road, it was dark, and while I knew the road during the day, I seemed blind to all the dents and bumps in the darkness. I was painfully aware of every bump and vibration for no other reason than knowing that I had nobody with me to support the cake, and it was now left to the grace of the road and my driving.

About a mile from the homestead, I stopped to do a damage assessment, and low and behold, it was only slightly skewed. 'Not bad,' I thought. It wasn't leaning over more than the Tower of Pisa, a global tourist attraction. The cake and I were about to arrive just fine.

Then tragedy struck. I could already see the light, so the house was within a short distance. Excitement was rising and perhaps I lost concentration, or maybe I sped up a little in my eagerness to pass on the responsibility of transporting the cake. Who could know? What I do know is that, out of the darkness, a deer suddenly appeared in the bright light of the headlamps. Emergency stop!

And the cake?

It was instantly disassembled. I looked down, almost too scared to see how bad it was and I saw three layers of soft and indulgent cake, smothered in soft dark chocolate mousse, laying spread across the floor on the passenger side of my car.

As much as I tried to deliver the cake in a state of perfection, my efforts were as much in vain as they would be to try and establish personal growth and transformation while incapable of effectively navigating the emotional challenges along the way.

Yet, there is a flip side to this statement: there is a lot of potential growth and transformation when you're able to navigate the emotional challenges along your way. I want us to explore the latter, as I want it to serve as encouragement to keep you going on this quest.

The Potential for Growth and Transformation Rooted in Emotional Navigation Skills

It was April 23, 1910, when Teddy Roosevelt delivered his Daring Greatly speech at the Sorbonne University in Paris.

I am sure you know the words of *The Man in the Arena*, as the speech is also often referred to.

"The credit belongs to the man who is actually in the arena, whose face is marred by dust and sweat and blood; who strives valiantly; who errs, who comes short again and again, because there is no effort without error and shortcoming... who at best knows in the end the triumph of high achievement, and who at worst, if he fails, at least fails while daring greatly..."[1]

At times, emotional growth and transformation may feel like you're losing in life. Yet, there are only two possible outcomes to expect: you're either going to end up victorious, being stronger, more confident, and more resilient than ever before, or you're going to fail, knowing you did so greatly. There are no losers in the quest for growth and expansion through developing your emotional management skills.

---

1   Brown, B. (2012). *Daring Greatly: How the Courage to Be Vulnerable Transforms the Way We live, love, parent, and Lead*. Gotham Books.

- *Greater emotional awareness.* Through increased emotional management through mindfulness practices like meditation, breathing exercises, journaling, and forging the mind-body connection, your awareness of your emotions becomes more vivid, allowing you to act in time before you get sucked into a state of negativity.

- *Increased confidence and self-esteem.* A sense of greater emotional control improves your self-esteem and expands your confidence in your ability to achieve your goals.

- *Know your strengths and weaknesses.* You are better equipped for self-reflection and can accurately identify your strengths and weaknesses without judgment. Through this simple acknowledgment of their existence, you have the foundation to expand on your strengths and strengthen your weaknesses.

- *Effectively portray empathy.* As your emotional management skills expand, you become better equipped to accurately recognize feelings in others, enabling you to portray empathy.

- *Enjoy stronger relationships.* Through increased understanding of the feelings others face and by offering effective support, your bonds grow stronger in these relationships.

Post-Traumatic Growth and Resilience

Post-traumatic growth (PTG) is the term used in psychology to refer to positive psychological change resulting from struggling and overcoming challenging and stressful life circumstances. PTG typically occurs in six stages, of which the initial stage is considered to establish the foundation from which you'll be operating.

- The foundation stage is primarily focused on establishing trust and connection with others who will be joining you on this recovery and growth journey.

- Stage 1 centers on education about your current state and the feelings it instills in you. It is all about acknowledging the pain you experience and how the battle you're in is impacting your life. But it is also about acknowledging and understanding that it is entirely normal and that similar challenges are part of life.

- Stage 2 focuses on regulation and cultivating calmness and clarity. It relies on mindfulness practices to encourage reflection. With this deeper understanding, it becomes easier to respond rationally and be more effective in navigating challenging feelings.

- Stage 3 is the disclosure stage, where now you feel comfortable sharing your traumatic experiences without feeling traumatized by doing so. It is the first indication of personal growth.

- Stage 4 is where you rebuild your story by picking up the pieces you want to keep and distancing yourself from the parts that no longer serve you. Now, you're rebuilding a better version of your life.

- Stage 5 is the service stage, where you've gained sufficient courage to share your story. You're strong enough to allow others to gain wisdom and insights from your painful experiences and that is how you enrich their lives.

A proper understanding of these stages of PTG can guide you along your healing journey, but what is even more important is knowing that it isn't only possible to heal and recover from exposure to hurtful and traumatic feelings, but you can also rise up much stronger than before.

Finding Meaning and Purpose Through Self-Reflection

Self-reflection allows you to get familiar with your traits and pain points. By practicing it regularly, you'll be able to recognize what works for you and what doesn't. From that understanding, it becomes easier to better plan your progress and to structure your personal growth practices to enjoy optimal growth.

There are multiple benefits to reap from regular self-reflection. Keep in mind that personal growth occurs when you take sustainable, small steps rather than trying to make major changes by taking big ones.

- *Self-reflection changes your perspective on life.* In moments of self-reflection, you gain distance from your situation. This distance allows a new perspective on the challenge you're facing and can reveal unexplored solutions. It also empowers you to re-evaluate your position in relation to your circumstances and the challenges that present.
- *You'll gain a greater understanding of yourself.* Self-reflection enables you to explore yourself from a distance and to do so objectively. It is how you get to know yourself better, making it easier to identify when your adaptive self is surfacing and how to replace that version of you with your authentic self.
- *Your life experiences will be more significant.* Self-reflection reveals your place and position in the greater scheme of life. It answers the need to belong to something larger than yourself. Finding your role in the large scheme of things adds significance to your life and meaning to your actions.
- *You'll find that life makes much more sense.* For as long as you're too close to your problems and challenges, it is hard to see beyond the problem, often leaving you with a sense of disillusionment. But once you gain a new perspective through self-reflection, life tends to make far more sense.
- *Your responses will improve.* In the absence of self-reflection, emotional management fades, allowing your feelings to direct your reaction to any external trigger. Through self-reflection, you'll gain control over

your emotions, enabling you to practice more effective emotional management so that you can respond effectively.

- ✧ *Your emotional management will become more effective.* One key benefit of self-reflection is an increased familiarity with your feelings. It enables you to acknowledge and confront your emotions to determine which feelings are justified and which are better resolved.
- ✧ *Your decision-making skills will get stronger.* Similar to your responses, you'll detect an improvement in your decision-making skills as self-reflection guides you toward making intellectual choices instead of emotional ones.
- ✧ *You'll know your purpose.* Purpose gives you a reason to get up after every tumble. It is what drives you amidst challenges and increases your resilience to keep going long after you've thought you're done. Self-reflection adds meaning and makes life so much more worthwhile.

In the end, it isn't just about knowing your purpose but also why it is your purpose and why you're exerting yourself in this manner. Nietzsche said, "He who has a why to live for can bear almost any how."[2]

---

2   Hicks, J., & King, L. (2021, November 2). *Three ways to see meaning in your life*. Greater Good. https://greatergood.berkeley.edu/article/item/three_ways_to_see_meaning_in_your_life

Ideas to Ponder

There is no denying that our emotions are extremely complex and intricate. Due to this complexity, it is so easy to get lost in all our feelings, and when this happens, every aspect of your life is impacted. But you don't have to remain in this negative state. The following points highlight the essence of how you can use mindfulness to let go of emotions that aren't serving you.

- We covered several helpful strategies to guide you from this state of emotional entrapment to a place of empowerment, enabling you to make sensible decisions and portray rational behavior.
- It explored how mindfulness practices can increase awareness, help you better identify your feelings, and guide you to process them effectively.
- We discovered how awareness of the mind-body connection enables you to use physical movement to process emotions.
- It expanded on how increased vulnerability is the key to authenticity, which in turn is the foundation of strong relationships while contributing to emotional resilience.
- It dug into how self-compassion can be cultivated in emotionally challenging times.

Lastly, we focused on the personal growth possible after post-traumatic experiences.

Conclusion

L etting go can be one of the easiest things you'll ever do.

But it is often one of the hardest things you may ever have to do.

This book serves as an exploration of the painful process of letting go. It explores the challenges of doing it, the obstacles you'll face, and offers guidelines on how to employ various strategies, with a specific focus on mindfulness exercises, to empower you to step into your freedom. We also explored the benefits you'll gain access to and the immense level of growth and self-development you'll be able to indulge in.

It is conveniently divided into six parts, each addressing a specific life area that is notoriously hard to let go of. But you can also read the entire book, as it serves as a guide to greater self-empowerment and as encouragement to improve your overall quality of life by following a more mindful approach to life.

- ✧ Part One focused on the past. We learned how you can recognize and resolve the toxicity resulting from trauma so that you can embrace freedom.
- ✧ Part Two shifted the focus to your external relationships and how these bonds can, at times, become bad for you. While the focus was predominantly on romantic relationships, it also contained several helpful strategies to ease the discomfort found in platonic bonds.

- ✧ In Part Three, we turned within to break the shackles of the inner critic. Doing so demands greater awareness of your internal chatter so that you can change the dialogue before a deeper sense of negativity sets in.
- ✧ Part Four explored the conflict we sometimes experience with our identity, and we discovered how important it is to get to know yourself and gain the confidence to stay true to your authentic self.
- ✧ In Part Five, we learned how to give up control through acceptance. It reminded us how important it is to identify what you can't change so that you can focus your limited resources on improving those things you can.
- ✧ Part Six focused on escaping the trap of entangled emotions and how to not only understand your emotional landscape but also how to utilize self-compassion and embrace vulnerability and authenticity.

Now, you're equipped to engage with life on a different level, to spread your wings in freedom, and to take flight into a better and more fulfilling future. You are empowered to pursue your purpose and have gained the emotional resilience to keep going until minor transformational steps turn into daily habits supporting and maintaining your personal growth.

I believe you have what it takes to let go and embrace your freedom, to continue your growth and to do so with self-compassion.

Often in life, the process of letting go is a continuous one, something you need to practice daily to secure your freedom. Continue to pursue this process, explore additional resources, and expand your knowledge and understanding of the strategies that support your quest to enjoy lasting emotional freedom, openness, curiosity, and authenticity.

Thank you for allowing me into your personal space and letting me be part of this intimate journey.

If you feel that this book and the strategies and practical exercises established the foundation for transformation in your life, share your experiences and pass on the key to ultimate freedom to many more to follow by leaving a positive review.

Printed in Great Britain
by Amazon